EDINBURGH ON A PLATE

First published 2000
By Black and White Publishing Ltd, Edinburgh
ISBN 1 902927 11 7
Introduction © Ferrier Richardson 2000
Text & Recipes © The Contributors 2000
Photographs © Alan Donaldson

British Library Cataloguing in Publication Data:
A catalogue record for this book is available
From the British Library.

The following Gary Rhodes recipes are reproduced by kind permission of the BBC:
Crispy bacon and egg salad from *New British Classics*, published 1999.
Onion and mushroom tart with a parsley garlic crust
from *More Rhodes Around Britain*, published 1995.

Project Manager: Siobhan Edwards

Printed in Spain by Bookprint S.L.

EDINBURGH ON A PLATE

EDITED BY
FERRIER RICHARDSON

PHOTOGRAPHS BY ALAN DONALDSON

CONTENTS

INTRODUCTION

Edinburgh over the last decade has developed into a city that 'reeks' of innovation and energy. Large operators and talented individuals have been weaving their magic wand, creating a plethora of wonderful restaurants and cafes from the West End down to the shores of Leith. The quality of establishments in Edinburgh – like all areas of Scotland – has improved dramatically, incorporating great design, great service, and great food. And, of course, having access to the best natural larder in the world, with wonderful game, beef, lamb and seafood, gives us an advantage over many other countries.

This wealth of natural ingredients and the abundance of visitors has encouraged a host of non-Scots to set up in Scotland's capital city, helping to create a melting pot of culinary embassies, and giving the city a very cosmopolitan feel.

Edinburgh on a Plate, like *Glasgow on a Plate* before it, represents the best in the city, and is intended to stimulate the reader to try these fantastic recipes at home. But even more, I hope the contents of each chapter will encourage you to dine in all these wonderful establishments, and see that – as well as all the beautiful historical sites, great art galleries and shops – Edinburgh's restaurants can bring a whole extra dimension to your visit or stay in this exciting city.

We have reproduced recipes as supplied by the chefs,
according to their own individual cooking style.
All recipes serve four, unless otherwise stated.

AJAY BHARTDWAJ

KALPNA

'I want to keep up to date with the modern flavours, but also to rediscover and revive traditional dishes.'

As a child, I was fascinated by food. I always wanted to know

what my mother was cooking, and how she made it taste good. When I decided to train in the catering business, I went to Delhi and started work in a restaurant, learning the basics. For sixteen years I worked in restaurants throughout India, learning to cook all different kinds of regional cuisine. And then I came to London and worked in the Mandeer in Tottenham Court Road. In 1982, I got offered the job of chef here at the Kalpna which was just opening. My wife didn't like Edinburgh much on our first visit (she found it too quiet), but we both love it now. Edinburgh is such a nice city; there is everything here, so much space, and it's so easy to get out to the countryside or to the mountains.

Kalpna is the only truly Indian vegetarian restaurant in Edinburgh. I come from Northern India and my wife, Neera, comes from Gujarat in Western India. We do all the preparation and cooking at Kalpna together. We go to India regularly – every year if we can. I like to try out food in the best hotels, but also in remote villages. I want to keep up to date with the modern flavours, but also to rediscover and revive traditional dishes. The food we serve here has a definite Indian philosophy behind it: the idea of three distinct types of food, for different types of people. Plain food is suitable for holy men and teachers, to help keep the body calm; spicy food for business people, to keep them alert, help them think and make them aggressive; meat for warriors, to make them hot blooded. Here we serve plain and spicy food, but no meat. We believe that food should be well-balanced, not harmful to the body. Sharp tastes are balanced with sweet and spicy flavours, to smooth and balance the food for digestion.

We have very loyal customers, people who have been coming to Kalpna since we opened. I always try out new dishes on customers, and I always want to know what they think. I think customers should complain if they are not happy with food – we try to give the customers what they want.

For *Edinburgh on a Plate* I have chosen simple dishes which are easy to make at home. The stuffed tomato dish is my own creation, and is an example of modern Indian cuisine; the pudding is very authentic, but much more simple than most Indian sweets.

FRUIT CHAT

2 small pineapples

1 green and red apple

110g white and red grapes

2 pears

2 bananas

1 kiwi fruit

10 strawberries

2 tbsp of sugar

3 tsp chat masala

   (you can buy this in any Indian shop)

$1/2$ tsp black pepper

1 tsp fresh lemon juice

2 tbsp chopped coriander

Cut pineapples in half lengthwise. Scoop out the flesh and remove the core. Cut the flesh in small pieces and place in a bowl.

Peel the fruit if desired and seed the grapes. Core and slice the apple, pears, kiwi, strawberries, and bananas and add to the pineapple with the grapes. Sprinkle with sugar, black pepper, chat masala, lemon juice and mix everything together. Leave the bowl covered, in a cool place until the sugar has dissolved.

Just before serving, pile the fruit back in the pineapple shells, and sprinkle with the finely chopped coriander. The remaining fruit may be offered separately.

CORN STUFFED TOMATOES

3 large tomatoes

250g or 1 medium tin of sweetcorn
(drain and crush some of the corn
before using)

2 small finely chopped onions

200g grated cheese

1 tbsp of lemon juice

1 tbsp of sugar

2 cloves of finely chopped garlic

2 tbsp of freshly chopped coriander

3 tbsp of freshly chopped mint

2 tbsp of oil

$^1/_2$ tsp of mustard seeds

$^1/_2$ tsp of finely chopped green chilli

$^1/_2$ tsp of finely chopped ginger

250g fresh cream

salt to taste

oil to deep fry the tomatoes

1 Cut the tops off the tomatoes. Scoop out the centres and drain the shells.

2 In the bowl put corn, onion, chilli, cheese and half the coriander mix them well.
Add lemon juice, sugar, and salt to taste, and mix.

3 Fill the tomatoes with the corn filling.

4 Heat the oil and then deep fry the filled tomatoes (you will see the skin coming off the tomatoes – take them out and put them in a serving plate).

For the Sauce

1 In the frying pan heat the oil.

2 Add the mustard seeds and as they start to pop add chopped ginger, garlic, fresh chopped mint and cream. Mix for two minutes.

3 Pour the sauce over the tomatoes and garnish with the remaining coriander.

ALOO BHAJI

1kg potatoes peeled, cut into cubes
   and boiled

3 green chilles finely chopped

3 diced tomatoes

1 tsp finely chopped garlic

1 tsp coriander and cumin powder

$1/2$ tsp chilli powder

$1/2$ tsp turmeric powder

$1/2$ tsp mustard seeds

$1/2$ tsp cumin seeds

4 tbsp of oil

$1/2$ bunch of finely chopped coriander
   for garnish

salt to taste

1 Heat the oil and add the cumin and mustard seeds until they pop.

2 Add the remaining ingredients, except the potatoes and cook for 2-3 minutes on medium heat.

3 Add the potatoes – mix well and cook for another 2-3 minutes.

4 Garnish with fresh coriander and serve.

AJAY BHARTDWAJ

GAJAR HALWA

1¹/₄kg grated carrots

570ml milk

250g sugar

250g ghee (purified or unsalted butter)

75g full cream milk powder

1 tsp cardamom powder

100g coarsely ground almonds and pistachios

Rose petals

1 Put the carrots and milk into a saucepan and bring it to the boil and keep stirring.

2 When the milk has evaporated, add butter or ghee and cook for 10 minutes stirring all the time.

3 Add sugar and cook for another 10-15 minutes on a medium heat.

4 Add the milk powder and cook for another 5 minutes. Mix everything well.

5 Add cardamom powder. Mix well.

6 Garnish with almonds, pistachios and rose petals.

ROY BRETT

MALMAISON

'Malmaison is all about the simple things done right.'

I've been working for Malmaison since day one – 1994 – and am now Executive Chef. I come from Edinburgh and trained at Telford College. My first job was at the Caledonian Hotel, where I worked for three years, before leaving to help out a friend – Wayne Bosworth – with the opening of a new hotel. I've worked with many great chefs over the years, but Wayne was probably the biggest influence on me, a chef who did his own thing, and thought of cooking as fun – it was great working with him. Tragically, Wayne was killed in a car crash in May this year; he will be much missed by me and his fellow chefs.

In the early 1990s, I'd been working at the Caprice in London and the Malmaison concept enticed me back to Scotland. I became Head Chef at the newly opened Malmaison Hotels in Glasgow and Edinburgh. Now I manage food standards and consistency in all the hotels, including menu writing, planning and development, recruiting chefs and training.

I spend a lot of my time travelling between the Malmaison Hotels in Leeds, Manchester and Newcastle, as well as Glasgow and Edinburgh; and next year there will be a new hotel in Birmingham and another in London to keep me busy. I am still very hands-on, cooking with my chefs four days a week. My role is to ensure that we have high standards that we can consistently meet – food that is good quality, and reliable, that customers really enjoy: Caesar Salad, steak frites, steak Béarnaise, and even prawn cocktail. I believe that restaurant food is for people to enjoy, not for the chef's sake. Malmaison is all about the simple things done right; we don't believe in reinventing the wheel. Our restaurants are very much based on the great French brasseries: stylish and serving well-prepared food at affordable prices. And family-friendly too – we like to cater for the tastes of the whole family, babies included. The Edinburgh Malmaison is in a great waterside location, and the building has real character – it used to be the Seaman's Institute, and still has a real maritime feel. The Head Chef is Stuart Muir, who was chef at the Glasgow Malmaison before coming here, and at the Balmoral before that. The food we've chosen comes straight from our chefs' recipe files and reflects the Malmaison style: full of flavour, with lots of French influences, particularly Provence and the Loire Valley. An honest and straightforward approach to good food.

ANTIPASTI

1 red pepper

1 baby aubergine

2 baby courgettes

1 fennel bulb

4 plum tomatoes

1 garlic bulb

60ml olive oil

1 sprig rosemary

1 sprig thyme

60g shaved Parmesan

20g capers

100ml salsa verdi

10g rock salt

To prepare tomatoes:

Put a base of rock salt on a baking tray. Cut tomatoes in half and place face up. Add thinly sliced garlic and olive oil. Season. Bake in a hot oven (200°C for 20 minutes). Once cooked, leave to dry at room temperature for 4 hours.

To prepare peppers:

Blister peppers under the grill, peel, deseed and cut into quarters.

To prepare other vegetables:

1 Cut the aubergine in half, and slice the courgettes at an angle.

2 Blanche the fennel.

3 Brush the aubergine, courgette and fennel with olive oil, and add rosemary and thyme.

4 Char-grill (under the grill), then season with salt and pepper.

5 Build the vegetables (including the roasted tomatoes and blistered peppers) in a pile in the centre of the plate, and cover with Parmesan shavings.

6 Finish with caper berries and salsa verdi (you can make salsa verdi with olive oil, capers and flat parsley or buy it ready-made in any good delicatessen).

FETA & ONION TARTE

4 sprigs chervil

2 large onions

40g butter

40g sugar

100g good quality puff pastry

100g Feta cheese

12 cherry tomatoes

4 tsp olive tapenade

10g rock salt

garlic

olive oil

To prepare tomatoes:

Put a base of rock salt on a baking tray. Place whole tomatoes face up. Add thinly sliced garlic, and olive oil. Season. Bake in a hot oven (200°C for 10 minutes). Once cooked, leave to dry at room temperature for 4 hours.

To prepare tarte:

1 Preheat the oven to 200°C.

2 Top and tail the onions and cut them in half. Put the onions in a non-stick blini pan with 10g butter and 10g sugar for each onion half. Place on a low heat and cook slowly until golden brown. Remove from the heat and allow to cool.

3 Roll out the puff pastry to make four discs 3mm thick and 130mm in diameter. Chill.

4 In each of four 10cm ramekins, place a pastry disc on top of an onion half. Fold the pastry disc over the sides of the dish. Bake in a preheated oven for 15-20 minutes, until the pastry is golden brown.

To present:

1 On each plate, place three baked tomatoes.

2 Turn out the tarte and pour over any juices from the blini pan.

3 Place a slice of Feta cheese on top and add a teaspoon of olive tapenade.

4 Garnish with chervil and serve immediately.

PROSCIUTTO WRAPPED CHICKEN

16 sprigs chervil

4 chicken breasts

4 slices prosciutto

100ml olive oil

200g butter

400g lentils (pre-soaked in
   cold water overnight)

800ml chicken stock

50g tarragon

To prepare lentils:

Bring chicken stock and lentils to the boil in a heavy-base pan. Cook thoroughly (for around 20 minutes). Fold in a little butter and chopped tarragon, cover in cling film and leave to infuse.

To prepare chicken:

1 Prepare each chicken breast by removing wing bone and discarding all skin and fat.

2 Season with salt and pepper, and wrap in a slice of prosciutto.

3 In a pan, heat a little olive oil and butter. Seal the wrapped chicken on both sides until golden brown.

4 Cook chicken in a hot oven (260°C), for 10-15 minutes.

To serve:

Place the chicken on top of the lentils.

Add four sprigs of chervil to each plate.

TRIFLE

200g rhubarb

2 large oranges

50g sugar

6 amaretti biscuits

200ml pastry cream

10g toasted almonds

Sherry

Pastry cream:

150ml milk

30g castor sugar

2 egg yolks

20g cornflour

200ml double cream

$^1/_2$ vanilla pod

To prepare pastry cream:

1 Bring the milk and vanilla pod to the boil in a heavy-based pan.

2 In a bowl, whisk together the egg yolks and sugar.

3 Pour the boiled milk into the eggs and sugar.

4 Fold in the cornflour.

5 Return the mixture to the pan and cook slowly on a low heat until the flour is completely cooked (the cooked mixture should coat the back of a spoon).

6 Allow to cool and add in the double cream.

To prepare trifle:

1 Cut the rhubarb into 2cm lengths and place flat on a baking tray with the orange juice, the zest of the oranges, and the sugar.

2 Bake at 150°C until soft and allow to cool.

3 Crush the amaretti biscuits and soak in sherry.

4 Line the bottom of a cocktail glass with the pastry cream mix, then cover with soaked amaretti biscuits.

5 Cover this with rhubarb and juice.

6 Cover with a little more pastry cream mix and continue to layer in this way until the glass is full.

7 Top with toasted almonds and serve.

IGGY CAMPOS

IGGS

'My aim is to make people feel at home, on familiar territory . . .'

I am Spanish – from Teruel – and came to Scotland

eighteen years ago. I have always been in the restaurant and hotel business, and have always loved food. I was brought up on a farm and used to come home from school to barefoot grape-crushing! I opened my first restaurant in Dundee; after a couple of years there, I worked my way around the north of Scotland and then came to Edinburgh to work at the Roxburghe Hotel. I found the right property and opened Iggs in 1989. This place is stylish, but relaxing; a good mixture – I think – of the formal and informal. The atmosphere is mellow. My aim is to make people feel at home, on familiar territory – we get lots of professional people here, lots of regulars, and we give them what they want. The service we offer is professional, but not too serious.

Most of our wine is Spanish and all the key Spanish ingredients – cheese, anchovies, spices and chorizo – come from Spain; for the rest we use good local produce. I get very excited by food – a trip round a supermarket is a real treat for me! I eat out as often as I can and all the time I'm noticing what other people do – what they cook, how they cook it, combinations, flavours, but also the style of the place, the service. I always check out the toilets too – these details are very important to the overall experience of visiting a restaurant. I go back to Spain often, too, and visit the best or newest restaurants in Barcelona.

My hero, in terms of cooking, is Marco Pierre White – he produces food that others have to follow. I love going to The Pharmacy in London, and Nobu; I love Japanese food. My ambition would be to run a restaurant with chefs cooking their national cuisine: Chinese, Indian, Japanese, African, French, Italian, and of course Spanish. I want Iggs to be known as one of the best restaurants in Scotland; it's not possible to be the best, but to always try to be better.

Andrew McQueen has been my chef here for the last two years. He was at the Sheraton for three years before this. The food we've chosen is very representative of what we do. Our ingredients and how we prepare them is often unexpected – mahi mahi steak, instead of cod or mackerel, and exotic fruit soup (a spicy and refreshing pudding). The starter of anchovies and tomatoes is my signature dish – it's simple, but so tasty, and it reminds me of my mother's cooking.

TOMATOES WITH ANCHOVIES

600g plum tomatoes

200g parsley

250g capers

120g anchovies (salted)

1 head garlic

570ml olive oil

crusty bread

1 Peel and chop the garlic.
2 Chop the parsley and slice the tomatoes quite thickly.
3 In an earthenware dish, lay one layer of tomatoes. Then sprinkle with garlic, parsley, capers and anchovies.
4 Repeat this process once more, then finish with a layer of tomatoes.
5 Cover with olive oil and place in the oven for about 20 minutes or until the tomatoes are very soft.
6 Serve with crusty bread.

VENISON LIVER

WITH SMOKED BACON AND ROASTED SWEET POTATO

500g venison liver

12 rashers smoked bacon

200g red onion

400g sweet potato

500g game stock

150ml sherry vinegar

200g Maris Piper potatoes

2 sprigs thyme

100g redcurrant jelly or honey

275ml red wine

2 cloves garlic (crushed)

50g butter

(Preparation is important in this dish so you have to start by making a red onion compote, then preparing the garnish).

1 Peel and slice the red onions then place them into a hot pan with a little olive oil.

2 Add the thyme, garlic and jelly, cook for about 5 minutes on a moderate heat, then add the red wine and cook slowly until the onion is very soft. (If the onion becomes dry during cooking add a bit of the meat stock.)

3 Peel potatoes and slice very thin, then cut the slices into thin straws.

4 Wash the straws in cold water to extract the starch, then deep fry until golden brown. These will be used for the garnish.

5 Now peel the sweet potato and slice about 1.5cm thick. Part cook in boiling salted water, then roast with a little butter in the oven on 190°C for about 10 minutes.

6 Now the only thing left is to make the sauce and cook the liver. Firstly, slice the liver and salt it. Put the liver in a very hot pan and cook for about 1 1/2 minutes on each side, then leave to rest.

7 In the same pan, cook the bacon and leave to rest.

8 Again in the same pan, add the game stock, bring it to the boil and reduce it by half. Now add the sherry vinegar and whisk in a little butter to give it a shine.

9 Assemble your dish on the plate, placing the four pieces of sweet potato in the middle, then, on top of that, put two spoons of onion compote. Now alternate three pieces of liver and smoked bacon, then spoon your rich sharp sauce over the top. Then garnish with the straws of crispy potato.

Photograph on page 19.

MAHI MAHI STEAK ON SAMPHIRE
WITH A CHIVE AND RED CAVIAR CREAM

200g x 4 mahi mahi steak (or any other firm white fish, e.g. shark)

1 punnet cherry tomatoes

400g samphire (seaweed)

400g Maris Piper potatoes

25g red caviar

25g chives (chopped)

275ml fish stock

150ml double cream

100g butter

A little olive oil

1 Peel and shape potatoes like small barrels, allowing 3 per person, then boil to cook.

2 Make the sauce by reducing the fish stock by half, then adding the cream; again reduce by a quarter. Now whisk in the butter being careful not to reboil the sauce, just keep it warm beside the cooker. If you do reboil it you will need to start again from the beginning!

3 Cut the cherry tomatoes in half and wash the samphire.

4 Put a little olive oil in a hot pan, salt the fish, then cook.

5 Sauté the samphire and cherry tomatoes, then place them in the middle of the serving plate. Arrange the potatoes around, then place the fish on top of the samphire.

6 Now add the caviar and chives to the fish cream and pour over the fish.

EXOTIC FRUIT SOUP

(This soup needs to be made the day before serving to get the best result.)

Ingredients for the Syrup

1 litre water

450g sugar

2 sticks cinnamon

1 vanilla pod

1 chilli

2 cardamon pods

2 tsp nutmeg

1 orange zest

1 lemon zest

Ingredients for the Fruit

1 mango

1 paw paw

$1/4$ pineapple

4 kiwi fruits

1 Dice all the fruit and place in a bowl.

2 Put all ingredients for the syrup into a pan and bring to the boil.

3 Now put all the fruit into the syrup and bring back to the boil, then take off the heat.

4 Return to the bowl and put into the fridge.

5 Serve as it is or with a sorbet or ice-cream.

CHRIS & GILL COLVERSON

LE CAFÉ ST HONORÉ

'A lot of the people who come here to eat are more like friends than customers.'

Chris and I met at Martins Restaurant where Chris was the chef and I was a waitress. I trained as a tapestry weaver at Edinburgh College of Art and worked as a waitress to support my studio work – I got commissions, but not quite enough to keep myself. Chris's career has been pretty varied too: he was in the Merchant Navy and then the Police; he played cricket a lot (in Yorkshire, where he comes from), and then he moved to Edinburgh and started in the kitchens at The Caledonian. The chef there at the time was Alan Hill; he was and is a huge influence. After The Caledonian, Chris went on to cook at Greywalls in Gullane, L'Auberge in Edinburgh and Gleneagles – again with Alan Hill. Chris has always been interested in cooking; at home they all mucked in and his Dad had three allotments so there was always plenty to cook! We love eating out, but we don't get that much chance when we're here. We go to Spain or Italy on our holidays and follow the locals; we come back and try things out, see what works.

We love Le Café St Honoré, the charm of the decor, the buzz and liveliness, and the intimate atmosphere of the place.

The food we serve is good, honest cooking. Fresh, full of flavour, and presented simply. The portions are hearty, which seems to go down well with everyone, particularly the business lunchers who come here regularly and with the rugby crowd – we always do very well when there are sporting events in Edinburgh.

We choose to be 'hands on' with our business and we try to offer a very personal service, with friendly staff; we've had the same team of staff for a long time and a lot of the people who come here to eat are more like friends than customers. We bake our own bread every day; our game comes from Aberdeenshire and the Borders; our fish comes from this great Chinese fish merchant in Marchmont, Eddie Kwok.

We are aware of possibilities of change in our future. Last Summer we took over Wigwam, a Mexican restaurant, just round the corner in Thistle Street. It's very different, but is proving a great success. It's been good to try something different and to let our staff move on – our sous chef set up Wigwam and the manager used to be a waiter here. It's great to have the new place so near, but it certainly helps to keep us busy!

GRILLED OYSTERS

BACON, SMOKED SALMON, HOLLANDAISE

12 oysters

8 bacon rashers

8 slices smoked salmon

salad leaves

4 lemon wedges

3 egg yolks

226g butter, melted

15ml white wine vinegar

15ml cold water

black, crushed peppercorns

1   Prepare oysters – you will need the twelve deeper shells, with an oyster in each – open oysters with oyster knife, inserting knife between shells at pointed end. Remove any broken shell, sever muscle at hinge if still attached and discard flatter shell half. Cover with damp cloth and place in fridge.

2   Grill bacon rashers till crispy and cut into fine slices.

3   To make the hollandaise, place egg yolks, cold water and vinegar in a pan over a bain marie or a pan half full of simmering water, whisk until egg yolks are smooth and thick. Whisk in melted butter a little at a time, until all butter has been absorbed and sauce looks thick and creamy.

4   To assemble, top oysters with bacon, coat with the hollandaise and grill under a hot grill till golden brown, approximately two minutes.

5   Arrange salad leaves and slices of smoked salmon on plates, add oyster shells and finish with a lemon wedge and crushed peppercorns to taste.

LAMB SHANK

GARLIC, SPINACH, BOUDIN NOIR

4 shanks of lamb

garlic bulb, peeled

root vegetables, roughly chopped:

   e.g. celeriac, parsnips, carrots, turnips

onion, chopped

2 medium boudin noir (black pudding)

1 bag spinach

1.2 litres lamb stock

bay leaves

flour

red wine

vegetable oil

olive oil

seasoning

1 Flour lamb shanks and seal in a hot pan with vegetable oil and seasoning, turning till a golden brown. Put shanks into an ovenproof casserole dish.

2 Pour off any fat from the sauté pan and add approximately $^1/_4$ bottle of red wine. Warm for a minute or two.

3 Put all root vegetables, onion, stock, bay leaf, garlic, red wine and seasoning into the casserole with the lamb shanks. Bring to the boil, cover and put into oven at 190ºC/375ºF, till tender. The cooking will take approximately two to three hours until the meat starts to fall off the bone. Keep the casserole covered, reducing the liquid slightly towards the end of the cooking time.

4 Whilst the lamb is cooking, wash the spinach thoroughly.

5 Just before serving, cut the boudin noir into chunky slices and grill. Wilt the spinach in a pan with olive oil.

6 To serve, place spinach in the centre of each plate, top with the lamb, spoon the sauce and vegetables around and finish with a few boudin noir slices.

Photograph on page 27.

PAN FRIED COD

WITH COCKLES & MUSSELS, CHILLIES AND SPRING ONION

4 cod portions, approx. 200g, filleted,
   with skin left on
mixture of fresh cockles and mussels in
   shells, 7/8 per person
1 green chilli, finely chopped
1 red chilli, finely chopped
1 bunch of spring onion, washed and
   chopped
olive oil
lemon wedges
seasoning

1 To prepare mussels, wash and de-beard (pull off wispy threads from shell) and discard any open or broken shells. Keep in fridge till ready to use.
2 To prepare cockles, soak for one hour in cold water. Scrub shells with cloth to remove grit and discard any open or broken shells. Keep in fridge until ready to use.
3 Heat olive oil in sauté pan till hot. Season cod and place skin side down in pan, cooking till golden brown. Turn fillets over, reduce heat slightly and cook over a medium heat. When almost cooked, nearly opaque in colour and firm, add mussels, spring onion and chillies. Adjust seasoning. Cover pan, cook till mussels open – approximately two minutes.
4 To serve, arrange cod fillets on each plate, pour over mussels and juices and garnish with lemon wedges.

LE CAFÉ ST HONORÉ CRÈME BRULÉE

6 eggs

1 pint/0.57 litres double cream

vanilla pod

75g castor sugar

castor sugar to dust tops of ramekins

small selection of fresh soft fruits

1 Separate egg yolks from whites.

2 Whisk egg yolks with sugar.

3 Split vanilla pod lengthways and place in a pan with the double cream. Bring slowly to a rolling boil and remove from heat.

4 Pour cream on to egg and sugar mixture stirring continuously.

5 Place pan over a medium heat, continuously stirring with a wooden spoon, till the mixture coats the back of the spoon. (Bring mixture to 83°C, no more.) Be careful not to allow the mixture to catch the bottom of the pan – to scramble. Remove immediately from the heat.

6 Pass mixture through a sieve and fill ramekin dishes. Allow to cool and place in fridge till set, preferably overnight.

7 To complete, top each ramekin with castor sugar, just enough to cover, and caramelise with either a blow torch or a very hot brulée iron.

8 Serve immediately with soft fruits as a garnish.

TIM CUMMING

THE VINTNERS ROOMS

'We put our energy and enthusiasm into obtaining the best ingredients, making everything ourselves.'

On leaving school, I balked at the thought of pursuing a life in estate agency, which a vocational guidance service had assessed as the career for me. Instead, I became a waiter at George Perry Smith's Hole in the Wall restaurant, in Bath. I loved it. The enthusiasm for real food underpinned everything. It was busy; this was the mid-sixties when there were very few genuine restaurants of worth, tourism was strong and eating out was becoming fashionable. Good food had always been part of family life: my mother is from Yorkshire, so Yorkshire Pudding was always perfect; my father, in between doctoring, found time to make game terrines – being in a rural practice, farmers would often produce pigeons, pheasants or hares. Life at The Hole in the Wall whetted my appetite, so I took a succession of jobs but none lived up to the integrity of The Hole, where I eventually secured a cooking position. After that, a restaurant of one's own became the obvious next step. Cranes Restaurant, in Salisbury, was started and ran for seven years through the late seventies with the blessing of the Good Food Guide 'Pestle and Mortar' and a Michelin Star. Another seven years rapidly disappeared in Bath – where The Hole had become available – before I finally took notice of my Uncle Charlie's pleas to look at the Vaults building in Leith. The ambience of The Vintners Rooms, with its mixture of formality and informality, and its wine trade history, made it hard to resist.

We want people to enjoy themselves, to feel happy and relaxed when they come here. Eating out is not just about the food on the plate, of course, but that bit must be right. We are not into messing with food, having too many competing flavours; rather we tend to be traditional, preferring tried and tested favourites and classic dishes, but not strictly so – while there are few combinations that have not been done before, we are always learning. We put our energy and enthusiasm into obtaining the best ingredients, making everything ourselves – not just the bread and ice creams, but black puddings, chorizo sausages, duck confits and so on. Our strongest influence is French provincial cooking in the vein of Elizabeth David and Jane Grigson, where the focus is on the worth and flavour of the essential ingredient. The food tends to be natural and honest, rather than fussy and over-elaborate.

CRAB & SHERRY TARTLET

1kg crab (or 220g fresh
   crab meat)
120g Gruyere cheese

Short Crust Pastry:
200g flour
150g butter
salt
iced water, approx. 100ml

Mushrooms:
120g button mushrooms
30g butter
100ml medium sherry
100ml cream
salt & pepper

Bechamel sauce:
30g butter
30g flour
200ml milk
200ml light stock (veg or
   fish)
1 tsp French mustard
salt & pepper

Crab preparation: Lightly scrub off any dirt or silt that is adhering to the crab.

Twist and remove all the claws. Lay the body on its back and prise out the central body part by levering from the rear using your thumbs. Discard the 'dead men's fingers' and the pointed flap. From the outer shell remove and discard any transparent membrane and the mouthpiece with its attached stomach sac. The mouthpiece is easily removed by pressing down, which will snap it away from the shell.

Scrape the brown meat from the shell into a bowl adding any brown meat from the central body part.

Into another bowl, using a shellfish pick or suitable sized teaspoon handle, pick all the white meat out of the cavities of the central part. Be very careful to avoid any shell. Divide the claws and legs into their different sections. Pick out all the white meat, cracking the pieces as necessary with a rolling pin or small mallet. Use just enough force to crack the shell and again be careful not to include any chips of shell.

Mushrooms: Soften in butter, add the sherry and reduce. Stir in cream, season and leave to cool.

Bechamel: Melt flour and butter and cook without browning. Add heated milk and stock bit by bit, beating until glossy between additions. Add mustard and seasoning.

Pastry: Sift the flour and salt into a bowl. Cut the butter into small cubes and add. Rub the butter into the flour using thumbs and fingertips until it forms small flakes like rolled oats. Add enough water to bind using a spoon. Form dough into a rough ball and keep cool (in fridge).

Roll out the pastry into 4 thin bases and place each in a greased, shallow and fluted flan ring (detachable base, 11cm by 2cm).

Cover with greaseproof paper or foil and weight with beans or rice, then place in a hot oven and bake for 10-15 minutes.

Once cool, trim off excess pastry from rim. Do not remove pastry from tins.

Spread in a good tablespoon of the mushroom/sherry mix.

Add 2 tablespoons of crab meat to each case and lightly season.

Mask with 2-3 tablespoons of the warmed bechamel sauce and a sprinkling of grated Gruyere and then bake in a hot oven for 10-15 minutes.

Remove from flan rings to serve.

Photograph on page 35.

BAKED TURBOT

WITH CHANTERELLES, THYME AND CHARDONNAY

4 fillets of skinned turbot (each weighing 200g)

50g butter

2 shallots finely chopped

180g local chanterelles

2 plum tomatoes, poached, seeded and sliced

4 sprigs thyme

100ml Chardonnay

100ml fish stock

salt pepper and lemon juice

4 tbsp double cream

Smear butter round a shallow, oven proof dish and sprinkle with shallots.

Put in the turbot fillets.

Strew around the mushrooms, slicing if too large.

Add the tomato, thyme, wine, stock and seasoning.

Cover loosely with a butter paper and bake for 10 minutes in a fairly hot oven (200°C).

When fish is just cooked, decant the liquor into a saucepan and reduce adding the cream. Check the seasoning, maybe sharpening with some lemon juice.

Arrange each fillet on a plate with the mushrooms and tomatoes, pour over the sauce and serve with new potatoes.

CACCIUCCO ALLA LIVORNESE

Fish of choice	1 bay leaf
2 tablespoons of olive oil	1 sprig parsley
1 onion	1 sprig thyme
1 carrot	$^1/_2$ star anise
1 stick of celery	500g fish bones
1 clove garlic	150ml red wine
1 chilli	1 or 2 squid ink sachets
Outer layer of bulb fennel	500ml fish stock
4 ripe tomatoes	croutons
salt and pepper	sauce rouille

Fry the roughly chopped onion, carrot, celery, chilli, garlic and fennel in the oil in suitable saucepan for a few minutes. Add the bay, parsley, thyme, star anise and the fish bones and fry for a few more minutes before adding the roughly chopped tomato and the red wine. Reduce the liquid by half, then add the stock and squid ink. Bring to the boil season and simmer for half an hour. Strain carefully through a fine mesh sieve.

When serving add appropriate fish and shellfish, such as lightly sautéed squid or cuttlefish, mussels, scallops, langoustines, little fillets of mullet or sea bass etc.

   Serve croutons and sauce rouille on the side.

BRANDY SNAP BASKET
WITH SUMMER FRUITS AND DRAMBUIE SYLLABUB

Brandy snaps:
30g butter
1 tbsp brown sugar
1 tbsp golden syrup
1 tbsp sieved flour
$1/4$ tsp ground ginger
scrape of nutmeg
grated rind $1/4$ lemon
1 tsp brandy

Drambuie syllabub:
grated rind and juice of
$1/2$ lemon
50g castor sugar
30ml Madeira
30ml Drambuie
130ml double cream

Summer fruits:
450g (total) of
raspberries,
strawberries,
blackcurrants and
redcurrants

Brandy snaps: Melt butter, brown sugar and golden syrup over a low heat. Combine the flour, ginger, nutmeg and lemon rind and warm through. Add to the syrup mix and finally stir in the brandy.

Space dessert spoonfuls of the mixture on a greaseproof-paper lined baking tray. Bake at 325°F, 170°C for 8-10 minutes.

Remove from oven and cool, but whilst still pliable place over upturned cups to form basket shapes.

Drambuie syllabub: Mix together the lemon juice and rind with the castor sugar, Madeira and Drambuie until the sugar has dissolved. Add the cream and whisk to soft peaks.

Layer the syllabub and fruits in the baskets ending with a garnish of redcurrants and a sprig of mint.

Photograph on page 41.

MALCOLM DUCK

DUCK'S AT LE MARCHÉ NOIR

'Good food, good wine and good people, that's what life is all about.'

I opened Le Marché Noir in 1989 with a

business partner, who ran it till 1991 when I left the Royal Marines. We parted company six months later and I have run it on my own for the last 9 years. I believe running a restaurant is very much a team exercise. It's about empowerment, allowing each person to do their job, with everybody pulling in the same direction. The individual may be good, but it's the combination that produces the magic. The same goes for food, wine, décor and staff. Good food, good wine, good service don't work on their own. Put them together, add people and stir! I don't believe in the modern fad that you have to be a chef to be a restaurateur. Most chefs know about food, but how many like people or understand wine and service? The restaurateur is the conductor, he has to be visible to the customer and care about all aspects of the operation. Duck's at Le Marché Noir is a relaxed yet formal restaurant; we aim to give customers what they want. I learnt about teamwork in the forces, and two other important things 'don't fail' and 'you can do it', crucial lessons in self-belief and motivation. I saw active service including the Falklands, which taught me to appreciate life; my main ambition is simply to enjoy today and hopefully be around tomorrow.

At Duck's we use the tremendous natural produce of Scotland, with French influences, in that the fundamentals of classic good cooking come from France. We pay a lot of attention to wine and its service, both new and old world. Our head chef, Brett Moremon, is Australian so our food definitely has Pacific Rim influences, but what matters is which flavours marry well with the produce.

I was the founding chairman of the Edinburgh Restaurateurs' Association and strongly believe that independent restaurants should work together and do more to get across the message to school kids, parents and students that catering can be a great career. It is immensely satisfying work and it is rewarding – there is money to be made.

I am a West Coast man and miss the Highlands, but I do love Edinburgh, the thinking man's London. It has everything you need in a city, including space, and I married an Edinburgh girl, Fiona. Once you have opened a restaurant like this you are pretty tied to it – I'm very hands on and wouldn't want it any other way. Good food, good wine and good people, that's what life is all about. What could be more natural?

NORI ROLLS IN A CRISPY BATTER
WITH PICKLED CUCUMBER, WASABI CREAM
AND ROCKET LEAVES
(CHEF: LYNNE MACLEAN)

For the rice:
250g sushi rice
375ml water
40ml mirin
20ml white wine vinegar
salt

For the filling:
1 red pepper
1 green pepper
1 carrot
1 courgette

For wrapping:
4 sheets nori (seaweed)
some water with a little
    sugar and mirin added

For batter:
1/2 cup plain flour
1/2 cup self raising flour
1/2 cup cornflour
250ml iced water

Pickled cucumber:
1/2 cucumber
1/2 cup sugar
1/4 cup white wine vinegar
1/4 cup water

Wasabi cream:
1 tbsp wasabi paste
100ml cream

All parts of this dish can be made in advance, although the batter is best made on the day.

For the batter, sift and mix all three flours together in a bowl. Slowly add the water into the middle whisking until smooth – should be of a medium viscosity.

For the cucumber, remove seeds and slice flesh into long thin strips. Boil sugar, water and vinegar, then allow to cool. Add cucumber and refrigerate.

For the wasabi cream, take a small amount of cream and add it to the wasabi, to make the paste a little wetter and easier to mix in. Simply whisk remaining cream until it is slightly thickened. Mix wasabi back into cream and season with a little salt and white pepper.

For the rice. Place rice, water, mirin and white wine vinegar into a thick-bottomed cooking vessel and bring to boil with a lid on, stirring once in a while. When the rice comes to the boil, stir more often to ensure even cooking and prevent it catching. Continue this until the rice is cooked and the liquid has mostly been absorbed. The rice will be sticky and coming off the side of the pot/saucepan, looking like it is bound with glue when it is ready. If the rice looks ready, but is still a little raw, just add a little more water. Once cooked, spread the rice on a tray lined with cling film so that it is rectangular in shape and about 1.5cm thick. Fan with a book or whatever is convenient, so long as it has a fanning effect, until the rice stops steaming. Cover with cling film and refrigerate.

Prepare the vegetables into long thin strips. Have water/mirin/sugar mix nearby for brushing the nori sheets with.

Cut the rice into rectangles of a size to fit the width of the nori sheet and about $2/3$ of its depth. Brush the nori sheet with water/mirin/sugar mix until it is nicely moistened. Place rice on nori. Make a trench along the centre with your finger, then place various bits of the prepared vegetables, alternating the colours in the trench (just a wee trench). Roll the nori nice and tight, keeping the vegetables in the centre, until you have a perfect nori roll.

Then, simply flour the nori, dip it in batter and deep fry for about 5 minutes. Drain, season with a little salt, trim the ends and cut at a diagonal, displaying its coloured inside. Drizzle wasabi cream around the plate, with pickled cucumber littered throughout, stand nori to attention and drop rocket leaves dressed with a little of the cucumber pickling solution in the centre.

Serve.

Photograph on page 45.

OVEN ROASTED HALIBUT FILLET

ON ROAST VEGETABLE SALAD WITH PUMPKIN SEED PESTO
(CHEF: BRETT MOREMON)

4 x 170g portions of halibut fillet

olive oil for frying

2 bulbs fennel

1 red onion

1 courgette

4 cloves garlic

5 branches thyme

salad leaves

For the pesto:

100ml olive oil

1/2 bunch basil

50g green pumpkin seeds

25g Parmesan cheese

1 clove garlic

For the pesto, place all ingredients in a food processor and blitz until medium fine.

For the roast vegetable salad (this can be done in advance and reheated), trim the tops off the fennel, clean the bottom – but do not remove the knot. Cut in half across the widest part, then into eighths. Crush the garlic cloves with the skin on. In a roasting dish, heat some oil. Add garlic and thyme. Add fennel. Season. Stir and brown a little on top of stove, then place in oven and cook at 370°F for about 15-20 minutes – or until just soft. Cut courgette in half lengthways, then into diagonal chunks. Pan-fry in oil, with a little seasoning, until softish. For the onion, simply drizzle some olive oil over the top, leaving it in the skin, and put in the oven on a dish. Cook until soft, about 20 minutes. When cooled, peel the onion and cut into quarters, removing the knot so the onion breaks into pieces. Mix into the fennel and add the courgette. When serving, simply reheat in the oven with a little oil, then mix in a bowl with some salad leaves and a little of the pesto.

For the fish, heat a pan till it is very hot add a little oil. Season the fish with salt and ground white pepper and fry skin side up first (note the skin has been removed). When the fillet is golden brown, turn it over so the skin side is down and place in the oven to finish cooking – duration of cooking depends on thickness of the fillet. During the initial frying period, under no circumstances allow the oil to flame. Flamed olive oil will leave grey residue on the fish – and give a tainted flavour to match.

To serve, arrange the vegetable salad in the centre of the plate, drizzle pesto around and place the halibut fillet on top.

BEEF FILLET ON RATATOUILLE

WITH CRISPY PARSNIP CURLS AND MUSTARD SAUCE
(CHEF: DAVID SCOULLER)

4 x 225g fillet steaks

1 parsnip

For the ratouille:

¹/₂ a white onion

2 cloves of garlic

1 aubergine

2 courgettes

4 tomatoes

1 tsp tomato paste

1¹/₂ tsp sugar

For the sauce:

100ml red wine jus

100ml double cream

1 tsp freshly chopped
   rosemary

1 tsp Arran mustard

For the ratatouille, first prepare the vegetables. Dice the aubergine and the courgettes, keeping separate. Fry the aubergine in a little olive oil, likewise the courgette, until lightly cooked. Grind the garlic into a paste and dice the onion. Sweat in a little olive oil. Add diced tomatoes, stir, then add the sugar and tomato paste. Cook this to a thick purée texture. Add in your aubergine and courgette, stir and season. This can be made in advance and reheated.

For the sauce, bring the red wine jus and cream to the boil separately and then add together. Add the rosemary and mustard. Stir.

For the parsnip curls, peel the skin off the parsnips. Discard the skin. Then continue peeling the parsnip into strips. Fry in oil until golden brown, drain on paper and season.

For the beef, heat a pan till very hot, season the meat, then seal in the pan. Cook to desired degree in an oven at 450°F. Allow to rest after cooking.

To serve, place ratatouille in the centre of the plate, park the beef on top, garnish with parsnip crisps and circle with mustard sauce.

WHITE CHOCOLATE PARFAIT
WITH COCOA SORBET
(CHEF: BRETT MOREMON)

For the parfait:

5 egg yolks

100g castor sugar

100ml water

250ml cream

250g white chocolate

For the sorbet:

250ml sugar syrup (equal sugar/water)

250ml sparkling mineral water

50g finest cocoa

For the sauce:

100g dark chocolate

50ml milk

40ml double cream

20g sugar

For the parfait, place sugar and water in a pot and boil to 110ºC, with the help of a saccharimeter. Whisk the egg yolks (in a machine) till light, while the sugar is on the go. When sugar reaches 110ºC, slowly add to the yolks while still whisking. Continue whisking until cool. Have chocolate melted and whisk into yolk mix. Also, have cream whisked and fold into chocolate/yolk/sugar mix. Pour into a rectangular mould. Freeze, at least overnight.

For the sorbet, heat the sugar syrup, and pour over the cocoa while mixing. Ensure there are no lumps. Add sparkling water. Preferably, churn in an ice cream machine. Otherwise, place in a plastic container in the freezer, stirring from time to time with a fork, until frozen.

For the sauce, boil milk, cream and sugar. Pour over chocolate, whisk until smooth. Chill, but serve just above chilled, so that it pours easily.

To serve, drizzle sauce over plate, slice parfait with a hot knife and place a ball of sorbet on top.

Photograph on page 51.

GAVIN & KAREN FERGUSON

SKIPPERS

'The food is mostly fish, and always fresh, with minimal extras.'

Skippers was one of the first restaurants in Leith and has been going for over twenty years. The restaurant is cosy and quaint, with a relaxed atmosphere. The walls are covered with pictures and trinkets collected over the years, and we are slowly putting our own stamp on the place by adding bits and pieces from our travels.

When Karen and I met at university in Newcastle we quickly discovered that we shared the same ambition – to own a restaurant. We thought it would take us years to get our own place and run it the way we wanted. Then, suddenly Skippers came on the market and we knew we had to go for it. We love Edinburgh, the restaurant has a great reputation, Karen celebrated her 18th birthday here and we introduced our respective parents to each other over a meal in Skippers, so we knew it was right. We took it over in January 1999 and haven't looked back!

We have many regular clients, both locals and business people, but we also attract a lot of tourists. Skippers had a winning formula, which we are building on. There is more competition in Leith now and eating habits are changing, so we need to serve exceptional fish and make it look appealing. The food is mostly fish, and always fresh, with minimal extras. Alongside dishes such as whole grilled lemon sole, traditional 'home-cooked' dishes like fish pie and apple crumble always sell well. We work closely with our chefs, who plan the menus daily. We have given them more autonomy than they had before, allowing them to be more creative, whilst keeping to their budget. Kerr Marrian has been at Skippers for over 6 years now and our other chef, Stuart Thrumble, worked here several years ago and has recently returned.

We try to create a happy, relaxed atmosphere both for our customers and staff – we spend a lot of time out front, chatting and making people feel at home. It's that kind of place – friendly. We employ our waiting staff on the basis that they are approachable and easy-going; we can train them to hold a plate, but it's not so easy to train someone to be friendly!

The recipes we have selected are representative of the Skippers menu – the monkfish and bacon kebab is always a best-seller. People are often scared of cooking fish and these recipes take a bit of effort, but they'll work. They look and sound good and we hope people will want to try them out for themselves.

GAVIN & KAREN FERGUSON

OAK SMOKED TROUT & LIME PÂTÉ

WITH HORSERADISH & MELBA BRIOCHE

2 fillets of smoked trout – skinless

juice of 1 lime

zest of $1/2$ lime

pinch of cracked black pepper

175g full fat Philadelphia cream cheese

100ml single cream

1 tsp of creamed horseradish

1 brioche loaf

Herbs:

dill, chives, flat parsley

In the mixer, blend trout, black pepper, horseradish, lime zest and lime juice* until smooth.

Using a spatula, scrape down from the sides of the bowl, to ensure everything is thoroughly blended.

Add cream cheese and blend again.

Scrape down and blend, this time slowly adding the single cream through a funnel until the pâté is the required texture.

Transfer to a bowl. Using a spatula, fold in the finely chopped herbs. Chill for 30 minutes, then serve.

For Melba Brioche: Cut brioche into thick slices and remove the crusts. Toast carefully under grill on both sides. Slice horizontally, i.e. halving the thickness and toast again.

Garnish dish with freshly grated horseradish and lime zest.

* To maximise juice, microwave lime, after zesting, for 10 seconds.

MONKFISH & BACON KEBABS
WITH MUSTARD & CHIVE CREAM SAUCE

Ideal for dinner parties as they can be completely made in advance

8 rashers smoked back bacon

2 350g fillets of monkfish

2 large red peppers

1 lemon

8 shallots

red char and mizuma salad leaves

4 metal skewers

Sauce:

1 tsp whole grain mustard

1 cup chicken stock

$1/2$ cup whipping cream

50ml white wine

knob butter

chives

Ask your fishmonger to skin the monkfish properly for you. Cut each fillet into 4 chunks, wrap each chunk with one rasher of bacon. Start wrapping with the wider end of the bacon, leaving the fatty end on the outside.

Cut and prepare lemon and red pepper (large chunks). Shallots should be trimmed but kept whole.

To skewer: Start with monkfish, then lemon, red pepper and shallot – twice on each skewer.

On a large hot, well-oiled tray, seal the kebabs on both sides and then cook in a preheated oven (200°C) for 10-12 minutes.

For sauce: Melt butter in a heavy-based pan, then slowly add the wine. Reduce for a few minutes, add mustard and then chicken stock. Reduce again to half the quantity and then add cream. Pour into a jug and sprinkle in finely chopped chives.

To serve: Sauce should be poured warm on to a bed of red char and mizuma salad leaves. Lay kebabs on the salad leaves and garnish with flat parsley.

Photograph on page 55.

DUO OF SEA BASS & SEA BREAM
WITH ROASTED RED PEPPER RELISH

2 fillets of sea bass – pin-boned

2 fillets of sea bream – pin-boned

2 large red peppers – trimmed and
   seeded

2 cloves of crushed garlic

1 tbsp white wine vinegar

chopped coriander

pinch of cracked black pepper

1/2 red chilli – seeded and chopped

2 spring onions – chopped

pinch of castor sugar

butter and olive oil for frying

Score the fillets on skin side twice – this will stop them from curling with heat.

Fry gently in 1/2 butter, 1/2 olive oil – skin side first, a few minutes on each side.

Relish: Chop red peppers and toss in a little olive oil, roast in preheated oven at 200°C for 10 minutes.

Allow to cool, then roughly blend with sugar, garlic, vinegar and red chilli.

Remove from blender and mix in black pepper, coriander and spring onions.

Serve with a wedge of lemon and curly parsley.

Handy hint: Quality of fish is paramount – clear eyes and bright colours. Always ask to see the whole fish before it is filleted.

BANANA & TOFFEE CHEESECAKE

2 200g packs of Abbey Crunch biscuits

100g unsalted butter

250g Philadelphia cream cheese

1 tin condensed milk

200ml whipped cream (measure prior to whipping)

3 ripe bananas

Garnish:

grated white and dark chocolate

sliced strawberry

Place tin of condensed milk, unopened, in large pan of boiling water and boil for 3 hours, to produce toffee.

Place biscuits in food processor and pulse until crumbly. Melt butter over low heat and pour over biscuits. Press into cheesecake tin and chill for 20 minutes.

Spoon toffee on to chilled biscuits and add chopped bananas on top.

Whip cream to ribbon stage. Beat cream cheese until soft, then fold into cream. Spread evenly on top of bananas and refrigerate for 4 hours.

Grate white and dark chocolate over to garnish.

This dish is typical of Skippers – simple, but decadent.

NEIL FORBES

ATRIUM

'My philosophy of food is "taste, taste, taste"; excellence in all things.'

I've only been at the Atrium since last

August, but I love it. I'd always liked the place, the relaxed but formal feel of it and, of course, the reputation for great food.

Andrew and Lisa Radford give me free rein to do what I like here – they are around and very involved, but they let me cook and manage my kitchen as I want. My philosophy of food is 'taste, taste, taste'; excellence in all things, the best ingredients, simply but perfectly cooked. All the contents have a purpose and meaning, and marry together well. I don't believe in the bully-boy chef approach; I like my kitchen to be a happy and relaxed place where we work hard, but also have a laugh. We work as a team *and* work hard.

I always knew I was going to be a chef. My uncle, grandfather and father were all chefs. I grew up in Pitlochry, where my dad was a chef at a local hotel. A cottage came with the job and we lived next door to the Head Chef. Then we moved to Aldershot, where my dad was a chef lecturer for the army. I always helped with outside catering jobs and, when I was old enough, got a job working in an Italian restaurant in Camberley. I'd only been cooking for 3 years when I applied for and got a job at the Peat Inn in Fife, working for David Wilson – David has been a great influence on me. When I worked for David, I was very competitive, struggling to work out what makes a 'real' chef, and was very focused on the big-name London chefs like Marco Pierre White; David was always encouraging me to learn from the classical French chefs and I realise now that David was right! One of my best experiences as a chef was working on the Royal Scotsman for three years. And I got some brilliant training in brief stints at Le Manoir, under Raymond Blanc, and with Michel Roux, as well as with Andrew Fairlie (of One Devonshire Gardens, Glasgow) who is now a good friend of mine.

I love working in Edinburgh – it's such a relaxed city, architecturally stunning and with great views. I don't want to work in London and I never want to stop being a chef. The major frustration of being a chef in Edinburgh is how to get hold of the best produce. So much of it gets sent straight to London, even though it comes from Scotland – outstanding stuff like mushrooms and scallops. We need the best here!

SEARED SCALLOPS, GLOBE ARTICHOKE AND CRAB SALAD
WITH DILL HOLLANDAISE AND DILL OIL

20 good size fresh scallops (removed
   from the shell and cleaned)
4 globe artichoke bottoms (peeled,
   cooked and trimmed)
4 tbsp fresh white crab meat
200g rocolla leaves
50g fresh dill (finely chopped)
4 tbsp fresh hollandaise sauce
100ml extra virgin olive oil
Maldon salt, fresh ground black pepper
juice of 1 lemon

In a large pan, wilt down the rocolla with a little of the olive oil. Season. Keep in a warm place. Warm the hollandaise sauce and add half the dill. On four warm flat plates, place the artichoke bottoms, in the centre of which put the fresh white crab meat. Blend the remaining dill with some of the olive oil and pass through a fine sieve.

Place a good iron frying pan on to heat, add a little olive oil and start to fry the scallops. Turn when golden brown, season and turn out of the pan on to a cloth. Drizzle with lemon juice.

Arrange around the artichoke and crab. Make four balls out of the rocolla and place on to the crab salad. Spoon some dill hollandaise on to the rocolla and drizzle the dill oil around the scallops. Serve.

BREAST OF GRESSINGHAM DUCK

BOK CHOI, STICKY BELLY PORK, LENTIL
AND CORIANDER SAUCE

4 breasts of Gressingham duck (trimmed and scored
   on the skin side)

4 bok choi heads

4 x 5cm pieces belly pork (skinned and braised until
   tender)

200g Puy lentils (cooked with bite)

50g chopped coriander (keep stalks for sauce)

1 litre duck stock

100ml red wine

100ml cherry brandy

zest of 1 orange

1 tsp redcurrant jelly

1 tsp Chinese five spice

100ml light soy sauce

100ml dark brown muscovado sugar

50g golden syrup

few sprigs thyme

2 cloves garlic

In a thick-bottomed pan, reduce the red wine, cherry brandy, orange zest and redcurrant jelly until they form a glaze. Pour in the duck stock. Add the coriander stalks and reduce by ⅔ until the flavour is developed and consistency is perfect. Leave in a warm place whilst you braise the pork pieces in water with the garlic and thyme (approximately 1 hour or until tender). Meanwhile fry the duck breasts, skin side down, in a hot frying pan until golden brown. Flip over, fry again and return to skin side. Cook in a moderate oven until medium rare. Season and allow to rest in a warm place. Roughly chop the bok choi and wilt down in a little oil with salt and pepper. Place on the top of four warmed plates. Heat the soy sauce, Chinese five spice, sugar and syrup in a pan. Pass the belly pork squares through the mix and place on to the bok choi. Slice the duck breast and fan the slices around the bottom of the plate. Add the lentils and chopped coriander to the sauce and drizzle around. Serve.

CRISP-SKINNED FILLET OF SALMON
RÖSTI POTATO, SPINACH AND WILD GARLIC,
OYSTER BEIGNETS

4 x 170g fillets of fresh salmon (scaled, pin-boned, skin on)

4 large Maris Piper potatoes (peeled)

200g fresh leaf spinach (picked and washed)

100g wild garlic leaves (picked and washed)

4 fresh oysters (removed from shell and lightly washed)

100g self-raising flour

enough beer to make a batter consistency

4 tbsp white wine sauce:

200ml white wine

200ml double cream

400ml extra virgin olive oil

Maldon salt and fresh ground pepper

4 large sprigs chervil

Grate the potatoes into a kitchen cloth. Season. Squeeze out all the juices. Divide between four warmed blini pans, press down with the back of a spoon until golden brown, then flip over. Repeat the process. When golden leave in a warm place.

Heat a thick-bottomed non-stick frying pan with a little oil. Place the salmon skin down and cook on a low heat until the skin is dark and crisp. Turn the salmon to colour the edges and the underside. Season with salt, pepper and lemon juice and set to one side. (Do not over-cook the salmon – it should be pink in the middle.)

In a small pot, place 100ml of the oil and heat to a temperature of 170°C. Make the batter by mixing the flour and enough of the beer to make a 'double cream' consistency. Season. Dip the oysters in the batter and fry until golden.

Heat a little oil in a large pot. Add the spinach and wild garlic. Season. Drain in a kitchen cloth.

To make the white wine sauce: Reduce the white wine in a thick-bottomed pan to syrup. Add double cream. Bring to boil, simmer and reduce until mixture has good pouring consistency. Season.

Put the rösti potato in the centre of each warm plate. Pile the spinach and wild garlic on top, then the salmon (skin side up) and finally the beignets and chervil. Drizzle warm white wine sauce around. Serve.

TARTE TATIN
CARAMEL ICE CREAM

For the tart

4 Granny Smith apples

160g unsalted butter

200g castor sugar

160g puff pastry

4 cast iron blini pans (very important)

For the ice cream

6 egg yolks

$^{1}/_{2}$ litre double cream

250g castor sugar

4 sprigs mint

icing sugar, to dust

Tart: Peel, quarter and core the apples. For this recipe use 5in blini pans. In the bottom of each pan place 40g of soft butter and 50g castor sugar. Add 3 of the quarters of apples and cook directly on the stove until dark and caramelised. Meanwhile roll out the puff pastry and cut into 5in diameter discs. Allow to rest. Once the apples have coloured sufficiently, allow to cool and refrigerate. Place the puff pastry on to the apples, tucking the pastry into the edges. Pierce two holes in the pastry top. Bake in a moderate oven (160°C). Leave to cool to let the pastry rest.

Caramel ice cream: In a thick-bottomed pan heat the double cream. Pour on to the egg yolks. Return to a clean pan and, over a low heat, stir until it coats the back of a spoon. Allow to cool. In a heavy-duty saucepan caramelise the sugar (the further caramelised and darker it is, the more bitter it will be). Add this sugar mix to the anglaise, stirring all the time. Allow to cool and churn in an ice cream machine.

Place the blini pans on to a fierce heat to melt the caramel. Turn out the tart on to the centre of a warmed plate, apple side up. Serve with the caramel ice cream, some fresh mint and a dusting of icing sugar.

RICHARD GLENNIE

CHANNINGS RESTAURANT

'I take my food very seriously, but I also believe that cooking should be fun.'

I've been chef at Channings for three years –

it was great to be made Head Chef at just 27. I come from Aberdeenshire and only really got into cooking because I didn't know what else to do at 16. I went to the careers office at school and they suggested cookery – it was that or car mechanics. As there is not much difference between the two, I thought 'what the heck' and went for cooking!

I went to college for a year in Aberdeen and then came south for my training: Borthwick Castle, Norton House, La Tante Claire in London (learning from Pierre Koffmann, but missing home too much to stay permanently). I then went to Dalmahoy where I worked with Malcolm Warham, who is now Head Chef at our sister restaurant 36 (how we enjoy giving his team there a thrashing at five-a-side football, when we have time!).

I take my food very seriously, but I also believe that cooking should be fun. We work in a stressful environment and I think that a tense team can lead to strained service, so I try to make everyone relax and have fun as much as possible. We have a young and enthusiastic staff; many of them have been at Channings for three years now, so our standards are consistently high, as is team morale.

My training as a chef has been predominantly classical and I use this as a firm basis for my own evolving style. I source natural produce and cook it simply, using classical flavours personalised with a modern, light touch – in keeping with the restaurant. We have a new Scandinavian-style conservatory dining area and modern wine bar, which are very light, bright and airy.

One of the most memorable moments for the team was achieving our second rosette within my first year here. One of my own favourite memories was serving our interpretation of a Scottish classic dish – deep-fried Mars bar and an Irn Bru sorbet! This raised a few eyebrows among the high profile diners at our Alternative Burns Night Supper!

The four recipes I have chosen are themed around the seasons. I prefer to use seasonal ingredients whenever possible and organic produce when it is available – luckily this is more and more. Happy cooking!

RICHARD GLENNIE

SEARED DIVER SCALLOPS
PICKLED YOUNG SPRING VEGETABLES,
PASTRY WAFERS AND ORGANIC LEAVES
AND HERBS

8 large scallops (cut in half)

4 baby fennel

8 baby carrots

8 baby leeks

2 large sheets of filo pastry

75ml of sauce vierge

selection of soft organic herbs and
    leaves

1 pickling bag full of spices

1 egg yolk

Sauce vierge

150ml olive oil

3 coriander seeds (crushed)

slice of garlic

1 shallot (chopped)

squeeze of lemon & orange

1 pkt of basil ($1/4$ reserved and cut into
    thin strips)

tomato (diced)

Maldon sea salt and pepper

1 **To make the sauce:** Warm the oil up with the shallot, garlic and crushed seeds and leave to infuse for 10 minutes. Cool completely.

2 Blitz the oil with the basil and juices and season.

3 Pass through muslin cloth and mix in the diced tomato and basil strips.

4 Brush the sheets of pastry with egg yolk and press together. Cut four rounds out and bake until golden brown.

5 Simmer the pickling bag with water, sugar and salt and cook the vegetables. Leave to cool in the liquid.

6 Heat a non-stick pan up, season and sear the scallops on both sides.

7 Season and dress the salad with a little of the sauce vierge.

8 Place two scallops in the centre of the plates. Start to build up the vegetables and salad with the pastry in between each layer.

9 Drizzle the sauce vierge around the plate.

SAUTÉ OF LOCAL VENISON

ON A CELERIAC FONDANT AND CONFIT CABBAGE, CANDIED
ROOTS AND POTATOES, DATE AND CHOCOLATE SAUCE

600g piece of venison
   saddle
12 small radishes
12 shallots
1 celeriac (cut into four
   round discs)
1 bag of baby spinach
2 large Maris Pipers (cut into
   12 rounds)
150g unsalted butter
Maldon sea salt and pepper
3 tbsps oil
$^1/_2$ litre of chicken stock

pinch of freshly grated
   nutmeg
cream

Confit Cabbage
$^1/_4$ small savoy cabbage
1 small carrot (sliced into
   strips)
1 small onion (sliced into
   strips)
$^1/_2$ clove garlic (crushed)
2 sprigs of thyme (chopped)
1 tbsp duck fat

Chocolate and date sauce
$^1/_4$ litre of light game stock
$^1/_4$ litre of brown chicken
   stock
1 knob of unsalted butter
30ml of Madeira
1 small piece of bitter
   chocolate
4 dates (chopped)

1 Heat a large black pan with one tablespoon of oil and 50g butter and gently caramelise the radishes and shallots. Add a small amount of stock and cook until tender. Repeat this method with both the celeriac and the potatoes (to make fondants).

2 Season the venison saddle and place into a hot pan with the remainder of the butter and gently sauté for 5-6 minutes. Rest the meat in a warm place.

3 Wilt the spinach down with a small amount of cream, nutmeg and seasoning. Keep warm.

4 Slice the venison and place on top of the confit cabbage and celeriac fondant. Surround the cabbage with the radishes and shallots and potatoes and drizzle the sauce round, top with the spinach.

Confit Cabbage

1 Sweat the onions, carrot, thyme and garlic in the duck fat.

2 Add the cabbage and season. Wilt the cabbage until cooked.

Chocolate and date sauce

Mix the two stocks and reduce the alcohol. Mix in the chocolate and dates and whisk in the butter.

Photograph on page 71.

FREE RANGE CHICKEN BREAST

SERVED ON CHANTERELLE RISOTTO,
ASPARAGUS RAVIOLI & SAUCE VIERGE

Risotto

150g arborio rice

800ml chicken stock (made with lots of
  mushroom trimmings)

3 finely chopped shallots

1 tbsp olive oil

1 tsp grated Parmesan

50g chanterelle mushrooms

100ml of Chardonnay

Maldon sea salt and pepper

Sauce Vierge

150ml olive oil

3 crushed coriander seeds

slice of garlic

1 shallot (chopped)

squeeze of lemon & orange

1 pkt of basil ($^1/_4$ reserved and cut into
  thin strips)

tomato (diced for garnish)

Maldon sea salt and pepper

Chicken Breast

4 breasts of chicken (with the fillets
  removed and reserved)

1 tbsp olive oil

knob of butter

Maldon sea salt and pepper

Asparagus Ravioli

4 chicken fillets (from the breasts)

8 asparagus sticks (cut into thirds)

100g pasta dough

50ml double cream

Maldon sea salt and pepper

Egg white

Pasta Dough

For 500g of dough:

250g sieved 00 grade Italian flour

1 large pinch of salt

2 whole medium eggs

3 egg yolks

1 tbsp of olive oil

Risotto

1 Gently heat the oil in a thick-based pan and sweat off the shallots for a couple of
   minutes.

2 Add the rice and coat with oil and cook for a minute. Deglaze by stirring in the wine
   to lift all the ingredients from the bottom of the pan.

3 Add the hot stock a ladle at a time, allowing it to evaporate in the rice before
   adding the next one. Continue to stir all the time.

4 Once the rice is cooked, but still has a bit of a nutty bite to it, drop in the

mushrooms, add the Parmesan and season to taste. It should look nice and creamy, not too wet.

Chicken Breast

1 Heat the olive oil and butter in a large black pan until the butter is foaming.

2 Season the breasts and fry skin side down first until golden brown and turn to seal the other side.

3 Place in a hot oven and cook for 10 minutes, basting all the time.

Sauce Vierge

1 Warm up the oil with the shallot, garlic and crushed seeds and leave to infuse for 10 minutes. Cool completely.

2 Blitz the oil with the basil and juices and season.

3 Pass through muslin cloth and mix in the diced tomato and basil strips.

Pasta Dough

Simply place all the ingredients into a food processor and blast for 2 minutes. Tip the dough onto a lightly floured surface and knead for a minute until it is completely together in a smooth ball. Divide up into pieces and freeze until needed.

Asparagus Ravioli

1 Boil the middles of the asparagus until soft but still green in colour and discard the bottom third. Refresh in cold water.

2 Process the chicken fillets and middles of the asparagus until a smooth paste is formed. Pulse in the cream, season and test a small amount of the raw chicken and asparagus mixture by dropping into boiling water and cooking through. Check seasoning. Pass through a fine mesh and leave for an hour.

3 Roll out the dough to mark 7 on your pasta machine and cut out 8 rounds.

4 Pipe on the mousse in the centre of 4 rounds. Brush the edges with egg white, stretch the lids over the tops and press firmly together.

5 Poach in salted water for 4 minutes.

To assemble the dish

1 Place a large cutter in the centre of a large plate and fill with risotto.

2 Slice the chicken breast around the top of the risotto.

3 Reheat the asparagus and ravioli and dress and season in the sauce vierge.

4 Place on top of chicken and drizzle with sauce vierge.

ICED ANISEED PARFAIT

WITH PISTACHIO PRALINE, BLUEBERRIES AND PERNOD

100g castor sugar

$^1/_2$ squeezed lemon

4 egg yolks

30ml Pernod

1 star anise (crushed)

300ml whipping cream

$^1/_4$ punnet of blueberries (or
blackberries)

Praline

150g shelled pistachios

100ml water

200g sugar

1 Make a syrup by boiling the sugar, lemon juice and star anise with a little water to 120°C. Sieve and cool slightly.

2 Cream the syrup, pernod and the egg yolks together until pale.

3 Lightly whip the cream and fold all ingredients together.

4 Freeze into four moulds wrapped in cling film for 3 hours.

Praline

1 Boil the water with the sugar until caramel stage is reached.

2 Mix in the nuts and turn out on to a slab.

3 Crush into a fine powder when it is cold.

4 Sprinkle the powder into templates and bake in a hot oven until remelted. Leave to cool.

Garnish with blueberries and syrup.

DAVID HAETZMAN

BLUE

'It's about enjoyable food, cooked simply and with flair.'

I've been at Blue since it opened three years ago. I was

working in Preston for Paul Heathcote; the job was great, modern relaxed, informal with the focus on good ingredients, but I wasn't wild about the place! I read an article about Andrew Radford's plans for opening Blue and approached him direct. My girlfriend Manda came with me as pastry chef and worked here full-time until she had our son, Alex, last year; she works here part-time now. Edinburgh is a great city, small, but cosmopolitan and friendly.

Andrew Radford has been a big influence on me, the kind of food he likes to cook, but more than that – the whole way of running a restaurant. The style of cooking at Blue is modern British, I suppose; it's about good quality food, but cheaper and maybe a bit more accessible than the Atrium, while aiming for the same standards. Our approach to work is informal and friendly. Particularly since I became a dad, but before that too, I believe that there is more to life than work. So I try to manage the kitchens here so that staff have time for their own life, and energy to give 100% when they are here. And we also want the place to be friendly for families, for mothers with babies, as well as for the business lunchers. The menu expands in the evening, and the food is a bit more intricate; we get pre-theatre diners, but also people through to 11 o'clock at night. I think I'm quite laid back, as Head Chefs go, and I don't believe in shouting at staff to make them work harder; it's hard to keep staff these days, so I try to work well with the good staff we've got. We have a great team of people now and we enjoy what we do; we're proud of what we put on each plate. We make as much we can on site – we bake our own bread, make our own pasta and ice cream. I'm very much against frozen food and very pro using small local suppliers as much as possible.

My ambitions are to keep on being busy and improving standards – there's always more to do and new and fresh ideas. One day, Manda and I would like to run our own restaurant with rooms, somewhere out of town, maybe in the Scottish Borders.

The recipes I've chosen are all about combining flavours that work well together, nothing whacky or unusual just for the sake of it. It's about enjoyable food, cooked simply and with flair.

CRISPY SALMON

BEAN SALAD, GUACAMOLE AND CRÈME FRAÎCHE

4 x 80g salmon fillets (skin on and
  scaled)

Guacamole
1 avocado
juice of 1 lime
1 red chilli (deseeded, finely chopped)

Bean salad
100g haricot beans (cooked)
100g black eye beans (cooked)
100g borlotti beans (cooked)
100g broad beans (cooked)
6 spring onions (sliced)
12 cherry tomatoes (quartered)
1 red pepper (skinned and diced)
1 tsp chopped coriander
juice of 1 lemon
50ml olive oil

Bean salad
Mix all the ingredients together. Season. Refrigerate for up to 6 hours before serving.

Guacamole
Remove skin and stone of the avocado. Blitz in food processor with lime and chilli. Season.

Assembly
In a very hot pan, sear the salmon for 1 minute on each side. Allow to rest for 2-3 minutes. Place the bean salad in a ring in the centre of the plate. Place salmon on top of beans. Place a spoonful of guacamole on the salmon and drizzle with crème fraîche. Serve.

ROAST RUMP OF LAMB
BUBBLE & SQUEAK, PEA PURÉE, BALSAMIC SHALLOT
DRESSING

4 x 170g lamb rumps

Bubble & Squeak

10 medium potatoes (peeled and cut into 4)

1 savoy cabbage (stalk removed and
   shredded)

1 onion (finely diced)

25g unsalted butter

50g chives (finely snipped)

Pea Purée

500g fresh peas

100ml rocket pesto

Balsamic Shallot Dressing

8 shallots (finely diced)

200ml good balsamic vinegar

200ml extra virgin olive oil

Bubble & Squeak

Place potatoes in pan of cold salted water. Bring to the boil and cook until soft. Drain well and set aside. Sweat off the cabbage and onion in butter in a hot pan for 2-3 minutes, keeping the cabbage as green as possible. Season. Mash the potatoes lightly. Add the cabbage mixture and chives. Season. Wrap the mixture in greaseproof paper and roll into a cylindrical shape. Place in fridge and allow to set, ideally leave overnight. Once set cut into cakes.

Pea Purée

Place the peas in a pan of salted boiling water. Simmer for 2 minutes and drain. Blitz in a food processor until smooth. Add rocket pesto. Season.

Balsamic Shallot Dressing

Place shallots and balsamic vinegar in a pan and reduce by a half. Allow to cool. Add olive oil and season.

Assembly

Seal lamb in a hot pan on each side and roast in a hot oven, over 220°C, for 7-8 minutes. Allow to rest. Lightly dust the bubble & squeak cake with seasoned flour and pan fry on both sides until golden brown and finish in a hot oven for 4-5 minutes. Place the cake at centre on a warmed bowl. Quenelle (create egg shape out of) pea purée with 2 large serving spoons and place next to cake. Carve lamb once and place on side. Drizzle dressing around plate. Serve.

Photograph on page 79.

D A V I D   H A E T Z M A N

PAN FRIED SEA BREAM

HORSERADISH BRIOCHE CRUST, TIAN OF MEDITTERANEAN VEGETABLES, FONDANT POTATO

4 x 170g fillets of sea
   bream
rocket leaves
chervil

Tian

2 courgettes (thinly sliced)
1 aubergine (thinly sliced)
4 plum tomatoes
   (blanched, peeled and
   thinly sliced)

Crust

200g brioche
2 tbsp horseradish sauce
sea salt
4 tbsp olive oil

Fondant potato

2 baking potatoes
100g butter
4 sprigs thyme
4 cloves garlic (crushed)

Beurre Blanc

2 shallots (peeled and
   sliced)
75ml white wine
75ml white wine vinegar
100ml cream (whipping or
   double)
200g cold butter (diced)

For the tian: Lightly brush a gallette mould (shallow metal dish) with olive oil and season. Place the courgette slices around the mould making sure the base of the mould is covered. Then place the tomato slices on top of the courgette. Dress the aubergine slices with a little olive oil to moisten, season and place on top of the tomato. Press the vegetables down firmly and bake in a medium/hot oven (150°C) for 6 minutes.

For the crust: Remove the brioche crusts. Blitz in a food processor. Add the horseradish and olive oil and season.

For the fondant potato: Peel the potatoes and cut into 5cm discs. Melt butter in a thick-bottomed pan. Seal potato discs on each side. Add thyme and garlic and bake in a medium oven (140°C) for 15 minutes until golden brown.

For the Beurre Blanc: In a small pan, place shallots, wine and vinegar on to a medium heat. Reduce until liquid has just about evaporated. Add cream and reduce by a half. Slowly whisk in butter. Once all butter has been incorporated season and pass through a fine strainer.

To assemble: Pan-fry bream in a pan with a little olive oil. Cook skin side down first. Turn after 2 minutes. Sprinkle crust over fish and place under a hot grill until crust browns. Place tian in the centre of a warmed plate. Put fondant potato on top of tian. Dress and season rocket leaves and place on potato. Place fish on top. Drizzle with beurre blanc. Garnish with chervil. Serve.

DAVID HAETZMAN

RHUBARB & CUSTARD SOUFFLÉ

APPLE CRUMBLE SORBET

Sorbet
6 apples (peeled and
    chopped)
100ml water
200ml stock syrup

Crumble
200g plain flour
100g soft butter
25g demerera sugar
25g castor sugar

Meringue
4 egg whites
225g castor sugar

Anglaise
125ml whipping/double
    cream
175ml milk
$^{1}/_{2}$ vanilla pod
8 egg yolks
75g castor sugar

Soufflé base
250g rhubarb (chopped)
50g castor sugar
150ml water
juice of 1 lemon
50g cornflour

Sorbet and Crumble: Stew the apples, water and 1 tablespoon of castor sugar. Meanwhile mix the crumble ingredients together by passing them through your fingers. Place on a lined baking tray and cook for 7-8 minutes until the crumble becomes crunchy. Break it up fairly roughly. Take off the apples, allow to cool, then add stock syrup and churn in ice cream machine. When the sorbet is finished churning, add chunks of crumble. Freeze.

Anglaise: Whisk together egg yolks and sugar until light. Boil the milk, cream and vanilla pod. Add the hot milk mixture to eggs and sugar. Whisk. Return to a clean pan and cook over a low heat until sauce coats back of a wooden spoon. Strain.

Soufflé base: Stew rhubarb with water, castor sugar and lemon for 15 minutes. Mix cornflour with cold water to make a smooth paste. Add to rhubarb, whisking constantly. Blitz in a food processor then pass through a medium strainer. Allow to cool.

Meringue: Whisk the egg whites to a soft peak. Add sugar gradually. Place rhubarb base into a bowl and fold in egg whites.

Assembly: Brush a $3^{1}/_{2}$ inch ramekin lightly with butter and then coat with sugar. Place the mixture into the ramekin, making sure that there are no air pockets. Smooth off the top and cook in a hot (220ºC) oven for 10 minutes. Serve on a plate with sorbet and a jug of the anglaise. When at the table insert a teaspoon into the top of the soufflé and pour in the crème anglaise.

DREW HERON & DAVID KINNES

THE POMPADOUR

'Although The Pompadour is a grand, fine-dining restaurant, the dishes are very simple and straightforward.'

DAVID: The Caledonian Hotel was opened in 1903 and was the original grand Edwardian station hotel in Edinburgh; before Waverley was built, the platform was at the back of the hotel. There are old photos in some of the hotel bedrooms of people getting off the trains, all dressed in their finery. We've recently been taken over by Hilton Hotels, which is a great opportunity for us, with extra investment and more staff; The Caledonian is Hilton's signature hotel in Scotland. In recent years, The Caledonian has moved far away from the old-style, stuffy hotel image and is more relaxed. The Pompadour was closed last year for 9 months for a complete refurbishment – it is a listed room so great care had to be taken; the Chinese-style wallpaper and the plaster-work are all hand-painted. I started work as an apprentice at the George Hotel here in Edinburgh, straight from school, and I've been head chef at the Craigellachie Hotel, in Speyside, and Rusacks Hotel and the Balbirnie House Hotel, both in Fife. I live in Fife and am a hugh fan of the great local restaurants. I know all the chefs and we often exchange ideas on food and recipes.

DREW: I have to admit I started pretty humbly as a chef, cooking chicken and chips and chicken in a basket for eight years! But then I started working with Ralph Porciani at Craigendarroch in Ballater, and followed him to the Balmoral here in Edinburgh. It was a very hard training, but I loved it. Ralph has been a massive influence on me; I love cooking great food. A few years after the Balmoral, I went down to the Grosvenor House Hotel in London, before coming to work at The Caledonian. It's great working here with David. He lets me do what I want, but also gives a lot of support. Although The Pompadour is a grand, fine-dining restaurant, the dishes are very simple and straightforward. I cook modern Scottish, but with lots of other influences; focusing on the flavours of the ingredients, bringing the flavours out. Nothing over-complicated. And the ingredients are top quality – a lot of the job is controlling quality. Our ambition is to win another rosette for The Pompadour – we have two rosettes already, but we want three. The dishes we have chosen for the book work together really well as a dinner party menu – it will blow your guests away!

DUO OF SEARED SCALLOPS AND LANGOUSTINE

FINE LEAVES AND BEETROOT VINAIGRETTE

6 diver caught king scallops (halved)

12 medium langoustines (shaped into rounds)

4 plush lollo rosso

4 plush radichio

4 plush oakleaf

4 plush fine frizzy

24 mache leaf (lamb's lettuce)

50g avocado (diced)

50g tomato concasse (coarsely chopped)

50g peppers (diced)

5ml champagne vinegar

3ml water

10g caviar

salt and pepper

10g coriander (chopped)

5ml lime juice

5g snippets of chives

4 sprigs plush chervil

5ml beetroot juice

40g beetroot brunoise (finely diced)

10ml olive oil

Avocado Salsa: Make avocado salsa by incorporating diced avocado, peppers, concasse, finely chopped coriander and lime juice. Season to taste and set aside.

Vinaigrette: Combine olive oil, champagne vinegar, water, beetroot juice, season to taste and add brunoise of beetroot.

Salad: To build raised salad, start with oakleaf, radichio, lollo, frizzy and snippets of chives and picked chervil. Set aside.

To plate: On a clean plate, place three symmetrical circles of avocado salsa using a no.3 cutter, in between place two mache leaves and, in between these, place a little caviar. In the centre, gently place the raised salad. Meanwhile pan-sear the scallop halves and langoustines, season well and place on to a piece of kitchen paper. Put the seared scallops on to the avocado salsa and place the langoustines just off mache leaves. Sprinkle with a little beetroot vinaigrette and serve at once.

MEDALLIONS OF ANGUS BEEF

ARTICHOKE PARCEL, CELERIAC
PURÉE, RED WINE MUSHROOM JUS

12 x 40g Angus beef rounds

120g celeriac purée

4 artichoke bottoms (blanched)

100g wild mushroom mousse

50g pig's caul

50g puff pastry (trellis marked)

12 quail eggs

12 turned new potato (shaped into
    barrels)

50ml garlic cream

20g button mushroom brunoise

10g chives (finely chopped)

5ml egg wash (egg and milk)

100ml red wine jus

Chicken mousse

100g chicken

150ml double cream

$1/2$ egg yolk

$1/2$ egg white

pinch salt and pepper

50g sautéed sliced wild mushroom

Chicken mousse: Blend chicken in a blender or food processor, add the eggs and blend. Season with a little salt, slowly blend in the double cream until you get a good consistency, season to taste and add the wild mushrooms.

Beef: Trim the beef fillet into a 3cm cylinder, wrap tightly in cling film for at least 24 hours, slice into 40g rounds.

Artichoke: Fill prepped artichoke bottoms with a little mushroom mousse, shape with a hot spoon into dome shape, cover with pig's caul and puff pastry trellis. Brush with a little egg wash. Bake at 200°C for 6 minutes and set aside in a warm place.

Potato: Boil turned new potato in the garlic cream, drain, sprinkle with chopped chives and set aside in a warm place.

Beef cooking: Season beef and seal well in a hot pan, roast 80% as required, rest in a warm place.

Quail eggs: In a rösti pan, gently fry the quail eggs and cut out with a no.3 cutter. Keep warm.

To plate: In the centre of a clean plate, place 1 artichoke parcel. At the top place 3 turned garlic potatoes and, at the bottom of the parcel, place 3 teaspoons of celeriac purée. Top with 3 beef medallions, then top the beef with the fried quail eggs. Add the mushroom brunoise to the jus and carefully spoon the jus around the plate. Serve at once.

TRANCHE OF HALIBUT
HERB CRUST, LANGOUSTINE TORTELLNI AND
BOUILLABAISSE SAUCE

4 x 125g halibut portions

8 halved baby fennel
(blanched)

8 asparagus tips
(blanched)

12 leaves of won ton
pastry

6 langoustines (shelled)

8g chopped mixed herbs
(chervil, dill, chives)

10ml shellfish oil

160g mashed potato

40g chopped lobster
(cooked)

Herb crust

100g unsalted butter

75g fresh breadcrumbs

100g chopped herbs

50g Gruyere cheese
(grated)

pinch salt and pepper

Tomato fondue

200g tomato flesh

10ml olive oil

5ml shellfish oil

sprig thyme

pinch salt and pepper

Shellfish oil

1kg lobster or
langoustine shells

2 litres vegetable oil

1 litre olive oil

200g tomato purée

2 garlic cloves

Bouillabaisse sauce

1/4 peeled potato

100g diced carrot

1/4 diced onion

100g diced celery

100g tomato purée

10ml brandy

1 litre fish stock

1 garlic clove

2 red mullet (gutted)

20ml olive oil

50ml double cream

pinch cayenne pepper

pinch saffron strands

salt and pepper

Herb crust: Blend all ingredients together in a blender or food processor. Place the mixture between 2 leaves of silicon paper and roll out until you get a 2mm thin sheet of crust. Chill in the fridge until set, cut into rectangles and keep cold.

Tomato fondue: In a pan, simmer all ingredients gently for 2 hours. Lift out thyme sprig and blend in a blender or food processor. Pass through a sieve and season to taste.

Bouillabaisse sauce: Marinade mullet, olive oil, cayenne and saffron for 24 hours. Roast all dry ingredients in a pan with a little olive oil, add the brandy and tomato purée, cover with fish stock and simmer for 1 hour. Blend and pass through a fine sieve. Bring to the boil and add in double cream, reduce by 1/3 and season to taste. Blend to a foam with a hand blender just before serving.

Shellfish oil: Put a little vegetable oil in a large hot pan, add clean shells and brown off. Add tomato purée, garlic clove and the rest of the oils. Simmer very slowly for 6 hours at the side of the stove, chill and pass through muslin cloth. You should end up with a light red shellfish oil.

Tortellini: Cut out won ton pastry into circle shapes with a no.6 cutter and wrap in cling film. Meanwhile chop the langoustines finely and bind in the chopped herbs with a little egg. Season to taste. Put a rounded portion of won ton paste just off centre and brush with a little water. Fold over and make tortellini shape and set aside in fridge.

Lobster mash: Mix chopped lobster and mashed potato, season to taste and keep warm.

Halibut: Season halibut and seal in a hot pan. Cook 80% and top with a little fondue and herb crust rectangle. Grill for 30 seconds and keep warm.

To plate: Blanch tortellini in a pan of boiling water and, in the centre of a warm clean plate, place some lobster mash. At the top of the plate, place 3 teaspoons of tomato fondue and place the tortellini on to the tomato fondue. Gently lay the halibut on to the lobster mash and garnish with baby fennel and asparagus tips. Spoon bouillabaisse around the plate, sprinkle with a little shellfish oil and serve at once.

Photograph on page 87.

DREW HERON & DAVID KINNES

ICED SOUFFLÉ OF DRAMBUIE

WITH MARMALADE SAUCE, FRESH RASPBERRIES AND CHOCOLATE

3 egg whites

125g castor sugar

90ml double cream

100g white sugar

10ml water

10ml Drambuie

80g quality marmalade

20ml stock syrup

16 orange segments

16 sprigs orange confit (from orange zest)

50g dark chocolate

10g icing sugar

1 Boil the water and white sugar until caramel, pour into a greased tray and cool. Blend until almost powder.

2 Prepare a meringue with egg whites and castor sugar. Semi-whip the double cream, fold meringue, caramel and Drambuie into double cream.

3 Pipe into prepared moulds. Freeze.

4 Meanwhile simmer marmalade and 10ml stock syrup and leave to cool. Add in a little water as it cools, until you get a good sauce consistency.

5 Add zest to 10ml of stock syrup. Bring to boil and cook for about 30 minutes to make sprigs of orange confit. Leave to cool.

6 Fillet oranges and caramelise segments with a little icing sugar.

7 Melt chocolate and pipe a square on each plate. Pipe a chocolate fence on to silicon paper, insert into a cutter, chill and remove silicon paper carefully.

8 To serve, spoon the marmalade sauce into chocolate square and at each corner place a raspberry and sprig of mint. In between place the orange segments and top with orange confit. Unmould soufflé and place in centre of the plate. Gently arrange chocolate fence around the soufflé. Dust with icing sugar and cocoa powder. Serve at once.

PELHAM HILL

RESTAURANT AT THE BONHAM

'I think of a restaurant as a theatre, a place for performance.'

I knew I was going to be a chef from about the age of nine. From the age of three, I lived in the Philipburn House Hotel which was owned and run by my parents. I started helping my dad in the kitchen as a very small boy, but my official training started when I was 15. I went to Hawick College and then on to Westminster College, when I worked front of house at Claridges. Back in Scotland, I decided I wanted to help my parents and worked with them until three years ago.

The Bonham is a big change. It's a solid, classical building with lots of original features with striking contemporary design features added. My style of cooking is similar, in a way. I use good basic ingredients – Scottish wherever possible – and combine them in a classical dish, but then do something different. I like the unexpected in cooking. The food here is Scottish 'with a twist'. I think of a restaurant as a theatre, a place for performance – I want diners at The Bonham to be challenged, pleasantly!

I suppose I am ambitious and although I am happy, I always want things to be better. Striving for improvement every day makes the job more stressful.

My aim here is to continue the success of The Bonham and to keep entertaining the diners. I've been strongly influenced by my parents and want to build up a reputation like they had. I'm not a big fan of celebrity chefs – they should spend more time in front of the stove! Having said that, I think my favourite restaurant in London was Aubergine, when Gordon Ramsay was there!

We get lots of celebrities here, but I train my staff to treat everyone the same. People don't want a fuss, they just want a good meal.

We had a strange request the other day from a woman who wanted the chocolate torte dessert as a starter – it seemed to make her happy. And she went on to have venison for her main course (no chocolate in this dish, although we do sometimes serve venison with chocolate couscous!).

Apart from the venison starter – which has been very popular ever since I tried it on the Christmas menu in 1998 – all the recipes I've chosen here are new. I like to experiment, try new combinations of tastes. I suppose I like living on the edge!

SALAD OF ROASTED VENISON
PARMESAN BISCUITS AND BABY LEEKS,
BALSAMIC DRESSING

600g venison fillet, cut into four

2 bunches baby leeks

salt and pepper

mixed salad: rocket leaves, basil,
    coriander and lamb's lettuce

olive oil with 8 year old balsamic vinegar

Parmesan biscuits

60g freshly grated Parmesan cheese

20g plain flour

10g cayenne pepper

pinch Maldon sea salt

1 Preheat oven to 200°C. Mix ingredients for biscuits together, shape, and place on a baking tray. Cook until golden brown. Cool on a wire rack.

2 Season venison with salt and pepper and seal in a frying pan before roasting in the oven for 10 minutes. Allow to cool.

3 Blanch leeks in boiling salted water for 2 minutes and refresh.

4 To serve, mix leaves with oil and balsamic and arrange in centre of plate. Slice each piece of venison into four, arrange on a plate, garnish with leeks and drizzle a little balsamic round the plate. Sprinkle with Maldon sea salt.

ROASTED ESCALOPE OF SEA BASS

TOMATO FONDUE, CABBAGE AND
PANCETTA MASH

4 x 200g sea bass

mustard (moutarde rustique)

For the tomato fondue

150ml olive oil

10 ripe plum tomatoes, skinned, seeded
and diced

4 shallots, peeled and finely chopped

3 garlic cloves, peeled and finely
chopped

2 sprig thyme

2 sprig rosemary

For the cabbage and pancetta mash

1kg spring cabbage

1kg Maris Piper potatoes, peeled

250g sliced pancetta (bacon), cut into
strips

150g soft Normandy butter

Maldon sea salt and pepper

For the tapenade

250g good quality pitted black olives

50g fresh anchovies

25g drained capers

2 cloves garlic

4 tbsp olive oil

1 For the mash, separate leaves from cabbage, cut away stalks and slice very thinly. Boil potatoes for about 20 minutes and drain. Blanch cabbage in boiling salted water for about 4 minutes and refresh. Pass potatoes through a ricer (a fine sieve), mix in butter, and leave cabbage and potatoes to stand.

2 For the tomato fondue, heat olive oil and sweat shallots and garlic without colouring. Add diced tomato, thyme and rosemary and cook until moisture from tomatoes has been removed. You should be left with a tomato paste. Remove herbs.

3 For the tapenade, blend all ingredients in a food processor for 5 min, then add oil.

4 Preheat oven to 200°C, smear sea bass fillets lightly with mustard, top with 1cm tomato fondue and place on a buttered paper on a baking sheet in the oven for 10 min.

5 Heat a saucepan with a little olive oil and add pancetta, crisp it up, add mash and fold in cabbage. Stir gently until heated through.

6 To serve, place mash in centre of a plate and place the sea bass on top and spoon a little tapenade round the plate.

OVEN BAKED RACK OF LAMB
SPICY SWEET POTATOES, MANGO & MINT SALSA

4 rack lamb, larder trimmed, skin
   removed and scored

2 large sweet potatoes, peeled and cut
   into 1cm slices (or new potatoes)

50ml toasted sesame oil

3 red chillies, deseeded and finely
   sliced

100g root ginger, cut into juliennes

200ml boiling water

50g coriander leaves

Maldon sea salt and pepper

Chervil to garnish

For the salsa

1 ripe but not over ripe mango

8 shallots, finely diced

50g mint leaves, shredded

juice and zest of 3 limes

1 red pepper, skinned, finely diced

4 plum tomatoes, skinned, finely diced

50ml olive oil

Maldon sea salt and pepper

1 Preheat oven to 200°C. Season lamb with salt and freshly ground black pepper and leave to stand for 45 minutes. In a bowl, mix potatoes, sesame oil, chillies and ginger. Place in a roasting dish, add boiling water and cook for about 30 minutes.

2 For the salsa, place all the ingredients in a bowl, mix together, cover bowl with cling film and leave at room temperature.

3 Heat a pan with a little sesame oil until almost smoking, seal the lamb on all sides and place in oven for 10 minutes.

4 Allow lamb to rest for 5 minutes.

5 To serve, add the chopped coriander to the sweet potato and arrange in the centre of the plate. Cut the rack of lamb into three pieces and place on the potato. Drizzle the salsa around the plate.

LIME, PASSION FRUIT AND COCONUT PARFAIT

For the parfait

6 egg yolks

150g castor sugar

25ml water

3 limes, zested and juiced

190ml double cream

150ml coconut milk

40ml Malibu

4 passion fruits

For the sauce

100ml lime juice

100g castor sugar

200ml water

2 passion fruits

$1/2$ fresh grated coconut

1   Mix egg yolks in a bowl with an electric whisk until thick and pale. Combine sugar and water and boil until it reaches 120°C. Slowly add the hot syrup to the egg mix, whisking all the time. Finally add lime zest and juice and passion fruit seeds.

2   Whip the cream to soft peaks and carefully fold in coconut milk. Then add egg mix and Malibu. Place in rings lined with cling film and freeze for at least 8 hours.

3   Place all the ingredients for the sauce in a pan and simmer until a syrup texture forms.

4   Shave the coconut with a potato peeler for garnish.

5   To serve, remove the parfait from the moulds and place on the syrup with the shavings on top.

Photograph on page 95.

MARTIN IRONS

MARTINS

'We feel very proud to be one of the longest established restaurants in Edinburgh.'

Gay and I opened Martins in June 1983. A continuation

of my career in hotels, inns and restaurants, and a diversion for Gay from fifteen years in health service administration. We started quietly with no advertising – a risk, considering our back-lane location. We relied on word of mouth recommendation, which is still true today, and now we can boast an international clientele, as well as entries in all the major food guides, and editorial in various food publications. In addition to our main dining room, we have two small private dining areas which are in constant demand by the business community, and also for special celebratory meals and family parties.

Our philosophy has evolved over the years, placing more emphasis on 'real' foods, fresh, local, properly sourced produce. We are active supporters of small food producers and use organic, wild and unpasteurised raw materials wherever possible. In the summer months, we use armfuls of fresh herbs from my father's garden in East Lothian. We are also active in campaigning against the deskilling of kitchens. I am a member of Eurotoques, a Europe-based lobbying movement to keep food fresh and 'real', and also of the Hospitality Industry Trust, a charity which raises bursaries for talented youngsters to help them further their career in the industry. We feel very proud to be one of the longest established restaurants in Edinburgh and to have had consecutive entries in the Consumers' Association Good Food Guide since 1985.

We have three highly talented chefs who, we believe, must have a platform to show off their skills. David Romanis, Head Chef, has been with us for three years. His style is about fresh tastes and flavours, allowing each to speak for itself. As part of our support for the 'artisan' cheesemaker, we have added a little 'theatre' to the dining room, with the presentation of the cheeses. This arouses interest from all the diners, not just those wishing to eat the cheese. Our style is 'Scottish rustic'. We hang our own game and lamb, as we like everything to be at its peak when we cook with it. The dishes we've chosen are particularly strong on flavours. The beef is from Stobo Farm, meat suppliers near Peebles – they supply us with beautiful free range lamb too. Traceability is everything these days, particularly with beef.

SEARED SCALLOPS AND LANGOUSTINE

ON A PICKLED VEGETABLE RELISH, CRISPY PARMA HAM
AND ROCKET LEAVES

12 fresh scallops

12 fresh langoustines

15ml olive oil

8 slices of parma ham

rocket leaves

For the relish

25g green pepper

25g red pepper

25g courgette

25g carrot

25g celery

$^1/_2$ red chilli

15g root ginger

juice of $^1/_2$ a lime

150ml white wine vinegar

30g fresh anchovy fillets

20g gherkins

20g capers

25g black olives

125ml olive oil

1 tsp chopped coriander

salt and pepper

Cut the peppers, courgette, carrot, celery, chilli and ginger into very fine dice, about 5mm square. Roughly chop the gherkins, capers, olives and anchovy. Mix all these together. Add the vinegar and lime juice and leave to marinate for 24 hours, stirring occasionally. Just before serving pour off most of the vinegar. Add the olive oil and coriander and season.

Remove scallops from the shells, clean and remove the coral. Peel the langoustine tails.

Season the shellfish and sear quickly in a hot pan for about 30 seconds each side.

Cut the parma ham slices into thin strips and deep fry with the rocket leaves for a few seconds until crispy.

Place the parma ham and rocket in the centre of 4 plates with the relish around. Put the shellfish on top.

PAN FRIED FILLET OF SEA BASS
BABY SPINACH, TARRAGON MASH, SHALLOTS, BACON AND
A DRY WHITE PORT SAUCE

4 fillets of sea bass (125g
   each)
20ml olive oil

For the mash
450g potatoes
75ml double cream
60g butter
2 tsp tarragon (chopped)

For the sauce
2 shallots (finely
   chopped)
150ml fish stock
100ml white wine
250ml double cream
30g butter
30ml dry white port

For the garnish
12 shallots (peeled but
   left whole)
150g bacon lardons
12 spears of baby
   asparagus
150g baby spinach
   (picked and washed)

Cook and mash the potatoes. Beat in the butter and cream. Add the tarragon and keep warm.

Blanch the shallots for 3 minutes, refresh and drain. Heat 15ml olive oil in a heavy frying pan. Add the shallots. Once they have started to colour and soften, add the bacon. Cook for a few minutes more, drain and keep warm.

To make the sauce, add the chopped shallots to the white wine and fish stock and put in a saucepan. Reduce until almost gone, add the cream and bring back to the boil. Add the dry white port and whisk in the butter. Pass through a fine sieve.

Quickly fry the sea bass in the hot olive oil for a couple of minutes each side.

Season the baby spinach and asparagus, steam for a minute, squeeze dry.

Put a circle of spinach in the centre of 4 warmed plates with a quenelle of mash on top. Spoon the sauce around with the shallots, bacon and asparagus. Place the pan-fried sea bass on top.

RIB EYE OF STOBO BEEF
HORSERADISH GRATIN, CELERIAC, MUSHROOMS, RED WINE AND THYME

4 rib eye steaks of Stobo
  beef (175g each)

For the gratin
400g potatoes
150ml milk
150ml double cream
1 clove of garlic (finely
  chopped)
25g grated fresh
  horseradish
salt and pepper

For the sauce
400ml veal stock
400ml brown chicken
  stock
250ml red wine
40g carrot
40g celery
40g shallots
10g fresh thyme

For the garnish
150g celeriac
100g mushrooms (pied
  blue, giroles or what is
  available)
80g broad beans

Wash, peel and slice the potatoes thinly. In a saucepan bring the milk and cream to the boil with the garlic. Add the sliced potatoes and the grated horseradish. Season with salt and pepper. Transfer to an ovenproof dish and cook at 180ºC for 30 minutes until golden.

Roughly chop the carrots, celery and shallots. Cook in a little oil in a hot saucepan until brown. Add half the thyme and the red wine and reduce until almost gone. Add the veal and brown chicken stock and reduce to about 15ml. Pass through a fine sieve and add the remaining picked thyme leaves.

Cut the celeriac into neat 2cm dice, blanch for 1 minute and refresh. Heat 15ml oil in a heavy frying pan, add celeriac and cook until golden and crisp. Pan-fry the mushrooms in a little butter.

Season the rib eye steaks and quickly cook on a hot chargrill for a few minutes each side. Allow to rest.

Spoon the horseradish gratin into the centre of 4 plates, arrange the celeriac and mushrooms around with a few steamed broad beans. Put the rib eye on top of the gratin and spoon the sauce over the meat.

GLAZED LEMON MOUSSE
WITH A SPICED ORANGE SYRUP

For the mousse

juice of 3 lemons

75ml double cream

3 eggs (separated)

18g flour

125g castor sugar

1¼ leaves of gelatine

For the syrup

200ml orange juice

100g castor sugar

¼ cinnamon stick

1 star anise

3 cloves

2 cardamon pods

½ pinch of saffron

¼ bay leaf

For the mousse, bring the lemon juice and cream to the boil in a saucepan. Beat the yolks with 25g of the sugar in a mixing bowl, along with the flour. Pour the cream on to the yolk mixture, mix well and return to the pan. Cook until thick and smooth. Add the gelatine and allow to cool.

Make an Italian Meringue by adding 100g castor sugar to 100ml cold water. Bring to 120°C, without stirring. Whip egg whites until stiff. Pour in hot sugar and continue whisking until mixture cools, and fold gently into the lemon custard mix. Spoon into 4cm round cutters and chill.

For the syrup, gently bring the orange juice and sugar to the boil, add all the other ingredients and reduce by about one half. Strain and cool.

Remove the mousses from the cutters, sprinkle with icing sugar and glaze with a blow torch or under a very hot grill. Put on to 4 plates and spoon the syrup around.

GEORGE & MICHELLE KELSO

HALDANES RESTAURANT

'We wanted to recreate the country house style in the city.'

Haldanes has been going for three years. Before that, we worked for ten years running Ardsheal House – a country house hotel in Argyll. We didn't know just how lucky we were there; the house was owned by a lovely American couple – Bob and Jane Taylor – and it was great having a captive audience. We had endless supplies of organic vegetables and herbs too!

When we came to Edinburgh and opened Haldanes we wanted to recreate the country house style in the city: a comfortable seating area with big sofas where guests relax and choose their food, and then three dining rooms. Spacious rooms, a fire, a garden. And, of course, food and service to enjoy. We were bucking the trend, really, it's the opposite of minimalism. An evening out with no rush – time to relax and enjoy. Affordable luxury.

It's taken a long time for us to get established, but we have managed it now. We get a lot of our business from word of mouth recommendation – people who come here for a business lunch or in a group and then bring back their partners, friends and family. That makes it all worthwhile – seeing guests come back again and again, knowing that they've enjoyed the experience. Our clientele is very mixed: visitors from other parts of Europe, American tourists, business people and regular locals.

The dishes we've chosen are very representative of what we do – 'modern Scottish' with strongly European influences. Light and simple. The best ingredients, not messed about – the dishes speak for themselves. We have lots of very popular dishes that we just can't take off the menu. The haggis is a real favourite. We didn't use to serve it, but one day (early on in our time here) a group of six Russians from a local hotel turned around and left when they found out we didn't serve haggis! We thought we'd better do something good with haggis straight away and have had it on the menu (in different forms) ever since. And the scallops always work too – simple and tasty. We still get our seafood direct from Argyll – it's so fresh and good, and we know the fishermen! The braised shank of lamb is a very meaty dish, real comfort food and great for a cold Edinburgh day. The lemon tart is Michelle's favourite – a classic dessert, sharp and delicate.

BAKED FILO OF TRADITIONAL HAGGIS
WITH ROASTED NEEPS AND A WHISKY SAUCE

1 small haggis of good quality

1 small yellow turnip

2 large sheets of filo pastry

2 tbsp of olive oil

seasoning to taste

melted butter

Sauce:

2 shallots finely chopped

25ml whisky

250ml veal/beef stock

seasoning to taste

Take the haggis, cook as per instructions and allow to cool. When cool make up 4 reasonable sized balls of haggis. Take 2 large sheets of filo pastry and butter lightly. Place together, one on top of the other, and cut to form 4 squares. Wrap the pastry around the haggis to form a parcel shape. Brush the pastry with melted butter. Bake in the oven for approximately 10 minutes, Gas Mark 6 (200ºC).

Neeps: Take a small yellow turnip, peel and dice into small cubes. Place in a pan of boiling water and cook until soft (not mushy). Take the turnip and shake off excess water. Place the cooked turnip on a baking tray with olive oil and roast for approximately 10 minutes.

Sauce: Gently sauté the shallots in a little melted butter until slightly soft and brown. Increase the heat and add the whisky to the shallots and flambé to reduce the alcohol. Add the stock and cook for a further 2-3 minutes. Pass through a sieve and season to taste.

To present: Spoon the roasted turnips on to the centre of a warmed plate. Place the haggis on top of the turnip. Pour around the sauce and garnish with a sprig of fresh herb.

Photograph on page 111.

SEARED SCALLOPS

WITH SMOKED BACON & LEEKS SERVED WITH A SAFFRON SAUCE & ROASTED CHERRY TOMATOES

20 medium (or 12 large) king scallops

1 large leek (finely chopped and
   blanched)

200ml fish stock

250ml double cream

50ml dry white wine

2 shallots (finely chopped)

12 cherry tomatoes

4 slices smoked bacon

tsp saffron powder (or a few strands)

seasoning to taste

Remove the orange roe from the scallops and allow to slightly dry off. Put tomatoes and bacon on a tray in a hot oven and cook until bacon is crispy and tomatoes are glazed. When cooked, keep warm but do not allow to cook any further. In a pan, reduce 50ml of the cream and add the blanched leeks and seasoning. Keep warm.

Sauce: Gently fry shallots, then add the fish stock, white wine and saffron. Reduce by half and add 200ml of the cream. Continue to cook until the sauce thickens. Strain and season to taste.

To serve: Sear the scallops lightly in hot oil and cook until slightly browned – approximately 30 seconds each side. Spoon the creamed leeks on to the centre of a warmed plate. Place scallops on plate around the leeks. Spoon the saffron sauce over the scallops and leeks – do not completely cover the scallops. Add the crispy bacon roughly sliced as a garnish and place the tomatoes around the scallops.

BRAISED SHANK OF SCOTTISH LAMB

4 shanks of lamb

1 tbsp olive oil

1 small onion, chopped

2 cloves of fresh garlic, skinned and
   sliced

2 medium carrots, chopped

4 sticks of celery, chopped

2 tbsp tomato purée

2 sprigs of rosemary, bruised

25g plain flour

1.2 litres of chicken stock/water

seasoning to taste

Garnish

4 large tbsp broad beans

2 tsp garlic purée

strand of fresh tarragon

250ml fresh double cream

seasoning to taste

Place a heavy-based roasting pan on the top of the stove. Place olive oil in pan and heat until very hot. Place shanks in the pan and brown them all over. When the shanks are browned, put all the chopped vegetables and garlic into the pan. Cook the vegetables until lightly brown – not burnt. Add tomato purée and cook until it all turns slightly brown in colour, then add the rosemary. Sprinkle the plain flour over the shanks and stir the mixture to distribute the flour evenly. Finally add the stock/water gradually until all the vegetables and stock are well mixed together. Cover the pan and all the ingredients with foil or a tight fitting lid and cook in a preheated oven Gas 4 (150°C), for approximately 1½ – 2 hours or until the meat appears to be very tender and falling away from the bone.

Broad bean garnish: Boil the cream, tarragon and garlic purée until slightly thickened, add blanched and peeled broad beans and remove from heat. Season to taste.

Sauce for lamb: Strain the cooking juices from the lamb into a heavy-based pot and reduce quickly. Season to taste.

To present: Place approximately 1 tablespoon of the beans on to the centre of a warmed plate. Take the shank and carefully position on top of the beans. Pour the sauce over the lamb.

CARAMELISED LEMON TART

Line a 6 inch (15mm) pastry flan top and sides with a thin shortcrust pastry and bake blind until lightly browned and firm to touch. Allow to cool. When cooled, sprinkle the lemon rind on the pastry base. Do not, at this stage, remove the pastry case from the tin.

Ingredients for filling:
juice and zest of 4 large lemons
165g of castor sugar
6 medium eggs
350ml double cream
small amount of icing sugar for glazing

Make up a syrup from the juice and castor sugar by folding the castor sugar into the juice and stirring slowly until the sugar is melted. Whisk the eggs and place in a cold pan. Pour double cream over the eggs in the pan and bring slowly to the boil. On a low heat, whisk in the lemon syrup. When well mixed together, pour the mixture through a fine sieve on to the pastry base which should be scattered with lemon rind. Bake the tart in a preheated oven at Gas Mark 4 (150°C) for approximately 40 minutes.

Remove from the oven and chill in a fridge until the mixture is well set.

To serve: Cut a chilled slice of the tart and dust with a little icing sugar. Using a blow-torch – if you have one – glaze the top very gently until the sugar melts and caramelises. You can also do this very slowly under a hot grill.

Serve with fresh berries or a fruit compote and a little crème fraîche or thick cream.

Photograph on page 115.

RACHAEL MacPHAIL

INDIGO YARD

'The style of food at Indigo Yard is based on modern European, with influences from nearly every corner of the globe.'

I am Executive Head Chef for Montpeliers Plc
– the company that owns Indigo Yard, Montpeliers in Bruntsfield and Iguana in Lothian Street. This summer will see me move to Rick's on Frederick Street – one of a new breed of venues, a bar/bistro with rooms. I'm really looking forward to this new challenge.

I've been a chef for 20 years and always knew this was what I wanted to do. Every summer when I was a child my sister and I went to stay with our grandparents in Tarbert on Loch Fyne. My grandfather was a fisherman who enjoyed hunting and growing all his own vegetables. My gran was always baking. She was a great cook – she used to cook in one of the grand manor houses when she was younger; everyone knew her and her cooking.

I've worked all over the place. My two years at Gleneagles were probably the hardest, but the best training. When I went there women chefs were a rarity. I had already been cooking for over two years and been to college, but the only job they offered me was in the 'cold' kitchen making sandwiches! I did that for a while, but kept on asking to work in the 'hot' kitchen and eventually they let me – I was the only girl there. After that I wanted to see the world, but again, as a woman, it was difficult to get work. So I went to work for the Sheraton when they opened in Edinburgh, and from there applied to work in the Sheraton in Perth – Australia not Scotland! I loved my two years in the sun, but I have to confess I missed the rain and the wonderful views in Edinburgh. I'm not from Edinburgh, but I love it.

The style of food at Indigo Yard is based on modern European, with influences from nearly every corner of the globe. The food is very fresh, and presentation is very important too. Indigo is stylish and popular, and the interior is modern, but using reclaimed materials – slates and bricks and all sorts – and there is a whole range of spaces which will suit different moods and different times of day or night. We're open from 8.30 in the morning through to late at night, so we have to offer a broad range of food – the dishes that I have chosen reflect this. My style of cooking food has been influenced by all the places I have worked in, but particularly Australia – the Thai influence on food is strong there. The sea bass dish is one of my inventions; I came up with it at home, based on what I had in the fridge and it works as well with other fish or chicken.

RACHAEL MacPHAIL

WHITE CRABMEAT SALAD
ON SHELLFISH SAUCE WITH ARTICHOKE CRISPS

350g white crabmeat	**Sauce**	**Garnish**
50ml olive oil	12 mussels	1 head Belgian endive
juice of 2 limes	12 clams	8 sprigs rocket
25g chopped chives	300ml mayonnaise	¹/₂ head lollo rosso
fresh ground pepper	50ml white wine	8 springs curly endive
salt	20ml lemon juice	1 whole artichoke

1 Squeeze crabmeat until dry (reserve liquid) and combine ingredients in a bowl adjusting seasoning to taste.

2 Steam mussels and clams in the white wine until well opened approximately 5 minutes. Drain liquid and reserve.

3 To make the sauce, place mayonnaise and reserved liquids in a mixing bowl and whisk until well combined. Add lemon juice and season to taste. The consistency should be fairly thin.

4 Peel artichoke by cutting away outer leaves and trim until only the bottom is left.

5 Slice thinly on a slicing machine or with a very sharp knife. The slices should be wafer thin.

6 Deep fry artichoke in hot oil until golden brown and crispy.

7 Wash and spin endive, lollo rosso and rocket and make a bouquet.

8 Place ring mould in the centre of the plate and push crabmeat into it. With the handle of a wooden spoon make a hole in the centre of the crab mix.

9 Place the bouquet of lettuce in the centre of the crabmeat and lift the ring off.

10 Place the artichoke (5 slices for each plate) in the salad bouquet.

11 Lastly drizzle shellfish sauce around the crabmeat salad and drizzle a little olive oil over the salad bouquet.

12 Place 3 mussels and 3 clams on sauce around crabmeat.

PAN FRIED SEA BASS

WITH ORIENTAL SAUCE ON LEAF SPINACH, CHERRY
TOMATOES AND BABY POTATOES

4 x 225g sea bass fillets

175g leaf spinach (picked and washed)

approximately 20 (depending on size)
baby new potatoes (boiled with skin on
and then cut in half)

1 red onion (peeled, cut in half and sliced)

1 punnet cherry tomatoes (washed and
stalks removed)

1 tbsp olive oil

1 carrot peeled (cut into ribbons and
fried)

Ingredients for sauce

100ml hoi sin sauce

100ml oyster sauce

50ml Chinese plum sauce

1 tsp fresh ginger, garlic, chilli, lemon
grass (chopped) or substitute lemon
grass with lemon juice

1 tbsp fresh coriander roughly chopped
(reserve a little for garnish)

100ml fish stock or water

1 Combine all ingredients for the sauce in a mixing bowl.

2 Seal the sea bass in a large frying pan with half the olive oil.

3 Remove the sea bass from pan and place on a baking tray. Continue cooking in a moderate oven (180°C) for 4-6 minutes depending on the size and thickness of the sea bass.

4 In pan used to cook the sea bass add remaining olive oil and sauté red onion and potatoes until golden brown.

5 Add sauce to frying pan and simmer for 1 minute. Add spinach and cherry tomatoes and cook for a another 1 minute.

6 Divide the cherry tomatoes, spinach and potato mixture between four warmed plates, reserving some of the sauce.

7 Place the sea bass on top and spoon over remaining sauce.

8 Garnish with a little chopped coriander and deep fried carrot ribbons.

SEARED LAMB RUMP

ON ROSEMARY AND SUNDRIED TOMATO POLENTA,
RATATOUILLE SAUCE AND RED ONION MARMALADE

4 x 180g lamb rump
   steaks

8 sundried tomatoes
$1/2$ oz chopped rosemary
   & 4 sprigs for garnish

50ml red wine
10g tomato purée
20ml olive oil

Polenta

880 ml of water

$1^{1}/_{4}$ cups polenta

salt and pepper

10g butter

$1/2$ cup of grated
   Parmesan

$1/2$ cup of Mascapone

Ratatouille

50g diced courgette

100g diced mixed
   peppers

50g diced aubergine

1 clove of garlic

50ml lamb stock

Red onion marmalade

225g sliced red onion

2oz 50g demerara sugar

25ml red wine

10ml vinegar

zest of 1 lemon

25g butter

Polenta

1 Put the water in a heavy-based pan over medium heat. Bring water to a slow simmer and slowly add polenta, whisking to combine. Cook on a low heat for 40-45 minutes, stirring from time to time. Polenta is cooked when it comes away from the sides of the pan.

2 Add remaining ingredients for the polenta and combine well. Taste and adjust seasoning if desired.

Ratatouille

Heat pan and add olive oil. Sauté courgettes, peppers, aubergine and garlic for 1-2 minutes. Add tomato purée and cook while stirring for another minute. Add red wine and lamb stock. Reduce to desired consistency and season to taste.

Red onion marmalade

Heat pan and add butter. Sauté onions and sugar until brown. Add remaining ingredients and reduce until thick and sticky.

Lamb and Assembly

1 Sear lamb in hot frying pan and continue to cook to desired degree. Remove lamb from pan and add ratatouille.

2 Place polenta onto four plates. Slice lamb and place on top of polenta.

3 Garnish with onion, marmalade and rosemary and drizzle ratatouille sauce around lamb.

Photograph on page 119.

INDIVIDUAL CARAMELISED LEMON AND ORANGE CHEESECAKE

ON ORANGE AND COINTREAU SYRUP

Bases

4½oz 125g digestive biscuits 7¼oz

2½oz 60g butter

pinch of ground cinnamon

5⁄8oz 15g demerara sugar

1½ eggs 7oz 200g castor sugar

30g castor sugar 25ml Cointreau

30g sour cream

½ lemon

2 oranges 7oz

½₂oz 10g cornflour and ½ tbsp
water mixed together

Filling

2¼oz 55g Philadelphia cream
cheese

2¼oz 55g ricotta cheese

Garnish

200g castor sugar

50ml double cream

icing sugar

mint leaves

Syrup

juice and zest of 4 oranges

Bases

1 Crush biscuits until they resemble breadcrumbs and add melted butter, cinnamon and demerara sugar. Combine well.

2 Place 4 ring moulds on a greased lined tray and divide biscuit mix between the 4 moulds. Press biscuit mix until the base is well covered.

Filling

1 Combine cream cheese, ricotta, castor sugar, eggs, sour cream, zest and juice of ½ lemon, zest of 2 oranges and cornflour. Mix in a bowl and beat until smooth.

2 Divide cheese mixture evenly between the 4 moulds.

3 Segment the other 2 oranges and lay the segments on top of the cheese mixture.

4 Bake in a moderate oven (180ºC) for 30-40 minutes.

Syrup

Place castor sugar, juice, orange zest and Cointreau in a pan and boil until thick and syrupy.

Garnish

1 Boil the castor sugar with a little water until it turns a dark golden colour (this is now caramel).

2 Take off the heat and allow to cool slightly.

3 Drizzle the caramel in a circling motion on to a greased tray (making 4 caramel shapes) and allow to set.

Assemble

1 Liberally dust cheesecakes with icing sugar and caramelise with blowtorch.

2 Place on plate and garnish with syrup, cream, mint and caramel shapes.

GARY RHODES

RHODES & CO.

'Affordable, informal dining in a relaxed, but stylish setting.'

I started life as a chef at the Amsterdam Hilton in 1979 after training at Thanet Technical College, in Broadstairs, Kent. Many years later, as Head Chef at the Castle Hotel in Taunton, I started to earn my culinary reputation by maintaining its Michelin star for over four years. My next stop was The Greenhouse restaurant, London (also achieving a Michelin star). It was during my time at The Greenhouse that I became more recognisable to the general public, after the first of my television series was broadcast.

Since opening the London restaurants – City Rhodes (which I opened with Gardner Merchant, now Sodexho, in 1997) and Rhodes in the Square (since 1998) – both restaurants have achieved Michelin status. The Edinburgh-based restaurant is the second Rhodes & Co. brasserie-style establishment that I, again with Sodexho, opened here in Rose Street in September 1999, following on from the success of the first Rhodes & Co. established in Manchester in February 1999. The Manchester brasserie is near the Man. United football ground; I'm a big football fan, which isn't difficult supporting Manchester United. Football and food . . . the perfect combination? What more could I ask?

The Rhodes & Co. concept has been developed with support from Sodexho and, in Edinburgh, we operate in association with the world-famous Jenners department store.

It's great to have a Rhodes & Co. in Edinburgh. This is my first venture in Scotland and I love this city – it's so lively and vibrant, one of the most exciting places in the United Kingdom and one of the fastest growing 'foodie' cities. The approach of the Rhodes & Co. brasseries is affordable, easy eating in a relaxed, but stylish setting. The décor, designed by David Collins (who also designed the Manchester restaurant), is contemporary, with dark oak, blue and brown leather seating, a glass staircase and bamboo features.

I was really proud when the Edinburgh Rhodes & Co. won the Michelin Bib Gourmand 2000 award – I felt very honoured to receive such an accolade and recognition only a few months after opening.

The dishes featured here are examples of the simplicity and fun that Rhodes & Co. represents, concentrating on great depth of flavour without overworking too many ingredients.

CRISPY BACON & EGG SALAD

4 slices of thick-sliced white, brown or
    granary bread, crusts removed
4-6 poached or soft-boiled eggs
4 rashers of thick-sliced back or streaky
    bacon
4 little gem lettuces, leaves separated
    and rinsed (2 small cos can also be
    used, tear the leaves into suitable
    strips)

3-4 tbsp red-wine vinegar
2-3 tbsp olive or groundnut oil
4 spring onions, washed and finely
    shredded
salt and pepper

Cut the slices of bread into 1cm dice, unless grilling. In this case, leave the slices
whole. Cut the soft-boiled eggs into quarters. The ingredients lists suggests 4-6 eggs
– 4 should be enough, but 6 eggs will obviously give more generous servings.

The bacon can now be pan-fried or grilled until crispy. If pan-frying, a dry pan can
be used – fat will be released into the pan from the bacon. This will also happen if
grilling. Whichever method you choose, keep the bacon fat for frying the bread. Once
cooked, remove the bacon from the pan and keep warm. Now add the bread and fry
until golden and crispy. You might need extra oil to achieve a golden finish. If the
bacon has been grilled, just brush each slice of bread with the fat released and toast.
Now it can be diced.

Season the salad leaves with salt and pepper. It's best, whenever making salads,
to sprinkle salt around the bowl and not directly on the leaves. This prevents the salt
from falling on to wet leaves and sticking in lumps. Cut the bacon into strips and mix
into the leaves, with the spring onions and fried/toasted bread. Mix together the red
wine vinegar and the olive/groundnut oil. This mixture should be spooned over the
leaves, adding just enough to coat. Arrange on four plates or present as one large
salad. The soft-boiled egg quarters can now also be seasoned with salt and pepper
and placed among the leaves.

For poached eggs, reheat in simmering water for 1 minute before placing on top of
the salad.

ROAST PORK FILLETS

ON BUTTERED CABBAGE WITH WILD MUSHROOMS

Sauce

450ml Noilly Prat (French dry vermouth)

300ml white wine preferably a
  Gewürtztraminer

juice of ¹/₂ lemon

175g finely sliced white button
  mushrooms

25-50g butter

4 large shallots, finely sliced

100-150ml double cream

4 x 175-200g trimmed, cleaned pork
  fillet portions

selection of chosen wild mushrooms

1 small savoy cabbage

salt and pepper

To finish

set soured cream

paprika

To make the sauce pour the Noilly Prat and white wine into two separate saucepans. Bring to the boil and reduce the Noilly Prat by half and the white wine by a third. Remove both from the heat and mix together. Squeeze the lemon juice on to the sliced mushrooms to keep them as white as possible. Melt 25g (1oz) of the butter in a saucepan and add the sliced shallots. Cook without colouring for a few minutes, until beginning to soften. Add the sliced mushrooms and continue to cook for a further 2-3 minutes.

The alcohol from the pans can now be added. On a low heat, simmer for 10-15 minutes. Add 100ml of the cream, return to the simmer and cook for a further minute before pushing through a sieve, leaving the remaining shallots and mushrooms totally dry. This will then mean that every last drop of juice and flavour has been extracted. The sauce can now be checked for seasoning with salt and pepper. It can then be finished with a little more cream and butter if needed.

Pan-fry the pork fillet to a medium degree and leave to rest before cooking the cabbage. Whilst the cabbage is cooking, lightly sauté the mushrooms in a pan with a knob of butter.

Quarter the cabbage, discarding any bruised outer leaves and cut away the core from each quarter. Cut into 1-2cm thick slices. Wash and drain well in a colander.

Melt a knob of butter in a large pan. Add the cabbage and cook on a medium heat, turning the cabbage carefully to ensure an even cooking. Any water from the cabbage will create its own steam that will cook the vegetable. Once tender, season with salt and pepper.

To present the dish, divide the cabbage between four plates or bowls, slice the pork fillet and dress along the cabbage. Spoon over the cooked mushrooms and pour sauce around. To finish the dish, add a teaspoon of set soured cream on top and dust with paprika.

ONION AND MUSHROOM TART
WITH A PARSLEY GARLIC CRUST

This tart cooks almost like a crumble with the garlic and parsley crust. It eats very well with a tomato salad or tomato and mustard seed salad.

Serves 6

25g unsalted butter

1 tbsp olive oil

4 onions, sliced

225g button mushrooms, sliced

salt and freshly ground black pepper

1 quantity Basic Tart Mix[*1]

6 x 10cm or 1 x 25cm puff pastry cases, blind baked

1/2 quantity Basic Crumble Mix[*2]

2 tbsp chopped fresh parsley

1 large garlic clove, crushed

Preheat the oven to Gas Mark 6/200°C.

Melt the butter with the olive oil, add the sliced onions and cook over a moderate heat for 2-3 minutes. Add the button mushrooms, increasing the heat, and cook for a further 2-3 minutes. Season with salt and pepper. Add the basic tart mix and cook without boiling for 15-20 minutes. The filling is now ready to use or it can also be cooled and kept chilled for a few days.

Spoon the mix into the cooked pastry cases and finish in the preheated oven for 15-20 minutes. One large flan will need 30-35 minutes.

While the tart is cooking, start to make the crumble topping. Add the crushed garlic to the shallots in the basic tart mix recipe and cook in the butter. Add the chopped parsley to the breadcrumbs and finish as per recipe.

Once the flans are cooked, sprinkle the parsley and garlic crust on top, covering the flan completely. Finish slowly under a grill until golden and crispy.

[*1]   **Basic tart mix**

This recipe has almost unlimited combinations. It also has to be one of the quickest and easiest tart mixes to make. The quantity of this basic recipe can easily be adjusted – it really depends on what the filling is going to be. This amount will be enough for six 10cm individual or one 25cm case.

Serves 6

300ml double cream

2 heaped tbsp freshly grated Parmesan

2 eggs, beaten

salt and freshly ground black pepper

Beat the cream, Parmesan and egg together and season with salt and pepper. The mix is now ready to use.

Almost any filling can be bound and finished with this mix, but all the fillings must be previously cooked or blanched before adding to the Parmesan cream. The filling can then be warmed until it thickens, making sure it does not boil as this will scramble the eggs. The mixture can then be spooned into tart cases and cooked in the oven until set, or chilled to be used later.

*2   Basic crumble mix

This recipe really could not be simpler. It's just two ingredients held together with butter and, of course, seasoned with salt and pepper. The nicest thing about it is that it lends itself to so many flavour combinations – from parsley and lemon to horseradish or mustard and herbs. If you are using additional flavours, add them before stirring in the shallot butter. All these flavours work well with fish, meat or vegetarian dishes.

It's best to use sliced bread that is 24 hours old, as this will firm the bread slightly and prevent the crumbs from becoming doughy.

Serves 4

6-8 slices white bread

2 large shallots or 1/2 onion, finely
    chopped

25-50g unsalted butter, melted

salt and freshly ground black pepper

Remove and discard the crusts from the bread and cut into quarters. The quickest way to turn these slices into crumbs is by blitzing in a food processor. If you do not have a food processor, simply rub the slices through a metal sieve.

Melt the butter with the chopped shallots and bring to a simmer, remove from the heat and leave to cool.

Gradually spoon some of the shallot butter into the crumbs, mixing all the time. The mix will be ready when it holds once pressed together, but it should still stay free-flowing.

GARY RHODES

PANCAKE 'FETTUCINI'
WITH A GRAND MARNIER
SUZETTE SAUCE

Serves 4-6

100g plain flour

pinch of salt

1 egg

300ml milk

25g unsalted butter

vegetable oil

Suzette Sauce

$^1/_2$ pint orange juice

zest of $^1/_2$ orange

juice of 1 lemon

2oz demerara sugar

$^1/_2$ tsp cornflour

3-4 tbsp Grand Marnier

Sift the flour and salt together. Beat the egg into the milk and whisk into the flour. Add the melted butter. The pancake mix is now ready.

Preheat a 20-25mm pancake pan (preferably square) and trickle some vegetable oil into the pan, making sure the oil has very lightly covered the pan. Add a thin layer of pancake mix to the pan. Cook for 15-20 seconds until lightly golden, then flip over and cook for a further 10-15 seconds on the other side. The pancake is now ready. Repeat the same process until all the mix is finished.

The pancakes can now be cut into 1cm thick strips to represent our homemade fettucini. Divide into 4 portions – these will now microwave when needed.

Suzette Sauce: Boil together the orange juice, lemon juice, orange zest and sugar and reduce by $^1/_3$. Loosen the cornflour with a drop of water, and thicken and whisk into the simmering juice to create a coating consistency. Finish with Grand Marnier to 'spice' the complete flavour of the sauce.

To finish: Place the reheated pancake pasta into separate bowls spooning the Grand Marnier suzette sauce over each.

Vanilla ice cream is a perfect accompaniment to this dish – alternatively a little homemade anglaise sauce/custard can be loosened with a drop of milk before warming and blitzing/liquidizing to a frothy milkshake consistency. This can now be spooned over each pile of pasta for a lighter finish to the dish.

DAVID HOWIE SCOTT

HOWIES

'It's great when people are surprised by the food and the price.'

Food is in my blood.

Even as a wee boy, I loved growing vegetables in the garden with my dad, and then digging them up and dragging them into the kitchen to prepare with my mum. During my school and university education I failed to get catering out of my system, always supplementing my student grant by working in various restaurants in Edinburgh. Despite myself, it was an enduring passion and, when I finished my Business Degree at Heriot Watt University – and after trying out a series of unfulfilling jobs – my original dream of opening my own restaurant kept coming back to me. So, in 1990, I took the plunge, opening what turned out to be the first Howies Restaurant.

It seems like a lifetime ago, as I have learned so much over the years. My priority has always been to employ talented and creative chefs, which in turn means Howies offers good quality food, value for money and approachability. It's great when people are surprised by the food and the price. I like beating expectations. The food has a solid core of Scottishness. I suppose the feel of the restaurants is French – casual smart. People come to Howies for the food, not the faff.

Each of the Howies restaurants is unique. There is no standard look or fit, which is why I am adamant they are not a 'chain'. We have an open culture here with staff being encouraged to speak up and contribute. They're allowed to make mistakes too! We've just been awarded 'Investors in People'; we are one of the very few independent restaurants in the country to win accreditation and we're very proud of it.

The dishes we have chosen are from the Howies dinner menu – the lunch menu tends to be less complex, lighter. These are a good representation of what we do. The beef and cod are Scottish and the Banana Tart Tatin is a Howies special – very popular. The recipes are from Scott Kirkham who has been with Howies for four years. Scott was a gamekeeper for four years before following his instinct into the kitchen, which may explain why (for the second year running) he is a finalist in the Taste of Scotland Lamb Challenge.

By the end of 2000 we hope to open our first restaurant outside Edinburgh.

CARPACCIO OF SCOTCH BEEF FILLET
PARMESAN CRACKLING, WALNUT OIL AND FINE HERBS

Beef

approximately 600g of Scotch
    beef fillet
5 tbsp each chopped parsley,
    chervil and chives
salt/pepper

Marinade

2 tbsp each chopped thyme,
    rosemary, sage and bay
2 tbsp each peppercorns,
    coriander seeds, sea salt,

cloves and dried mushrooms
enough sherry and olive oil in equal
    quantities to cover the beef

Parmesan crackling

approximately 200g of grated
    fresh Parmesan

Herb salad

bunches of red chard, endive,
    chive tips, chervil sprigs and
    basil tips

To marinade:

Cover the beef fillet in the marinade, preferably overnight.

To prepare the beef:

1 Remove beef from marinade and pat dry.
2 Season beef and carefully sear it in a hot pan on all sides until golden brown.
3 Lay out a double thickness of cling film large enough to place beef in the middle
   and leave 6 inches all around.
4 Roll beef in chopped chives, parsley and chervil covering all over.
5 Place in cling film, roll into tight parcel, tie ends to resemble a Christmas cracker.
6 Place into freezer until partly frozen – this will enable you to slice it as thinly as
   possible with a sharp knife – then place in fridge.

To prepare the crackling:

1 Place Parmesan in four circles, about 3 inches across, on a non-stick oven mat.
2 Put into a very hot oven for about 3-4 minutes or until just starting to golden round
   the edges.
3 Remove from oven and carefully lay over a rolling pin letting them set.

To serve:

Lay about 4 thin slices of beef round a plate to cover the bottom. Place some herb
salad in the centre of the beef. Drizzle with walnut oil, Maldon sea salt and cracked
pepper, then garnish with Parmesan.

CRISPY FILLET OF COD

WARM SPICED POTATO, SPINACH AND RED ONION SALAD
AND CORIANDER OIL

Cod

4 pieces of cod fillet (skin on) about
    200-225g each
flour for dusting (seasoned with sea salt
    and black pepper)
butter

Coriander oil

Blitz:

    bunch of coriander

    olive oil

    lemon juice

    salt/pepper

Spiced potato salad

About 20 new potatoes (par-boiled and
    quartered)
200g baby spinach leaves (washed)
1 red onion (finely sliced)
2 garlic cloves (crushed)
1 tsp crushed ginger
1 tsp turmeric
$1/2$ tsp cumin seeds
$1/2$ tsp curry powder
1 tbsp chopped mint
salt/pepper
clarified butter

To prepare cod:

1   Toss pieces of cod in seasoned flour and pat excess off.
2   Heat pan with a little oil and fry cod, skin side first, adding a little butter as it is
    cooking, until golden brown on all sides.
3   Remove from heat and rest in a warm place for 5 minutes.

To prepare potato salad:

1   Fry onion in clarified butter until soft.
2   Add potatoes and cook until golden.
3   Add all spices, ginger and garlic and cook for further 3-4 minutes.
4   Add spinach and mint and mix in until spinach has wilted.
5   Remove from heat.

To serve:

Place a ring in the centre of each plate and fill with warm potato salad, place cod on
top and drizzle with coriander oil.

At the restaurant we serve this with a rocket salad tossed in natural yoghurt vinaigrette.

Photograph on page 135.

CONFIT LEG OF DUCKLING

POTATO PURÉE, CRISPY FRIED CARROT SHAVINGS
AND AN ORANGE AND THYME GLAZE

Confit of duck

4 duck legs about 8oz each (bone
  trimmed of knuckle)

about 150g of sea salt

2 onions (quartered)

7 garlic cloves (crushed)

1 carrot (halved)

few sprigs of thyme and rosemary

2 bay leaves

1 star anise

few coriander seeds

few peppercorns

650g duck/goose fat (melted)

Potato purée

about 15 medium sized Maris Piper
  potatoes (peeled and quartered)

milk

salt/pepper

Crispy carrot

2 large carrots

oil for frying

Orange and thyme glaze

400ml fresh orange juice

250ml reduced chicken stock

$1/4$ vanilla pod

2 tbsp fresh thyme

1 tsp treacle

To prepare duck:

1 Rub duck legs in sea salt and leave in fridge for about 2 hours to help tenderise.

2 Remove legs from fridge, wash off excess salt and pat dry.

3 Place all ingredients in a tray deep enough for duck legs and cover with duck fat.

4 Place in preheated oven 150°C/gas mark 2/3 for about 2 hours.

5 Remove from oven and cool in duck fat until needed.

To prepare purée:

1 Boil potatoes in salted water until cooked through.

2 Strain off water, return to pan, cover and leave to steam.

3 Pass potato through a sieve into a bowl using the back of a spoon.

4 Season with salt and pepper and slowly beat in milk until creamy and drops from
  spoon.

5 Check seasoning.

To prepare carrots:

1 Peel carrots and slice lengthways into thin strips.

2 Blanch in boiling water and refresh in iced water, then pat dry.

3 Deep fry in hot oil until starting to go golden at the edges.

4 Remove and drain on kitchen paper.

To prepare glaze:

1 Reduce orange juice to a syrup.

2 Add chicken stock, seeds from vanilla pod and thyme leaves and reduce until coating the back of a spoon.

3 Finish with 1 tsp treacle and season with salt and pepper.

To serve:

1 Remove duck legs from fat and fry in a pan until crispy and brown.

2 Make a ring of potato purée in the centre of each plate.

3 Place a duck leg in the centre of the purée, glaze with orange and garnish with crispy carrot and fresh thyme leaves.

DAVID HOWIE SCOTT

BANANA TART TATIN
WITH CLOTTED CREAM AND CARAMEL SPRING

6 bananas (very firm)

50g unsalted butter

100g castor sugar

4 sheets ready-made puff pastry

1 tub clotted cream

1 Make a caramel with sugar and butter and pour into four individual pans or one larger pan.

2 Slice banana into 2.5cm pieces and place end up into the caramel circling the pan.

3 Roll each sheet of puff pastry to about 1.5mm thick and lay over banana tucking into pan around the edge.

4 Dust with icing sugar and bake at 220°C/gas mark 7 for 15 minutes.

5 Remove from oven and turn out on to plate banana up (watching out for the caramel – it's hot!)

We serve with clotted cream, mint and a caramel spring.

Caramel Springs

1 Cover the base of a small saucepan in about 5mm of castor sugar and place on a moderate heat.

2 Allow the sugar to melt until it reaches a 'hazelnut' or golden colour, making sure all the sugar has dissolved. Then dip the bottom of the pan in cold water, stopping the caramel from colouring any more.

3 As the caramel cools, take a spoon and dip it in and out again letting the caramel run off the spoon, then touch it against a steel and wind round and up the shaft of the steel in a spiral motion.

4 Once you reach the end of the steel, carefully pull the spoon away and slide off your spring on to a non-stick surface.

5 Repeat the process for the number of springs you need, but work quickly or the cooling caramel will become too bristle to work with.

JOHN & STEPHANIE TSE

THE BAMBOO GARDEN

'Eating out as a family should be a good experience.'

We were both born in Hong Kong. My brother

Henry came to Scotland in the 1960s to study at Edinburgh University; he liked the place so much, he stayed and in 1985 opened the Bamboo Garden. I studied Pharmacology at Liverpool University and was working for Glaxo (in the Marketing Department) in Hong Kong when my brother offered me the chance to take over the restaurant – he wanted to move on. He now owns Henry's Jazz Bar and a noodle restaurant here in Edinburgh. Stephanie worked with me at Glaxo and we decided to take cookery courses in Hong Kong and move to Scotland. We took over the restaurant in 1995. Stephanie is trained as a dim sum chef and still cooks all the dim sum we serve here.

We like Edinburgh very much. The people are very friendly, and the air and water are so clean – very different from Hong Kong! We do find it cold, but we are getting used to it. We love running a restaurant – meeting people, making new friends. We like entertaining people. We get lots of regular customers here, as well as tourists – Bamboo Garden is recommended in the Japanese Guide to Edinburgh, so we have many Japanese customers. This is a Hong Kong style Chinese restaurant, combining the best of all the provincial dishes. We go back to Hong Kong at least once a year, but sadly not often together – one of us goes for a fortnight or so, while the other one runs the restaurant. It's good to go and find out what's new there. A lot has changed since the end of British rule. The thing we miss most about Hong Kong is the produce – it is difficult to get hold of the quality of supplies we need here sometimes.

Our ambition is simply to serve the best Chinese food in town. The style here is casual, not fine-dining. We want people to relax and enjoy themselves. Eating out as a family should be a good experience (and good value for money). Probably the biggest influence was my father, who was the NAAFI manager for the British Forces in Hong Kong, before he opened his own restaurant. I was brought up in a restaurant. Good food was a daily thing.

The dishes we have chosen include our most popular ingredients; we specialise in fresh, local seafood such as seabass. The duck always goes down well, particularly with our many Chinese customers.

PEKING DUCK

duck (2-2.5kg)	**For pancakes**
maltose (15g)	white flour (300g)
malt vinegar (75g)	water (400g)
water (15ml)	salt ($1/2$ tsp)
(these 3 to be mixed together)	hoi-sin sauce
	shredded leek

Duck

Clean the duck before inserting a bamboo stick inside. Hook up duck and pour boiling water over it repeatedly until the skin shrinks. Rub vinegar and maltose mixture all over the duck. Air dry or blow dry using a fan. Roast the duck vertically in medium heat for 30 minutes. Skin and serve with pancakes, hoi-sin sauce and shredded leek.

Pancakes

Boil water with salt. Stir in the flour, mixing thoroughly, and cover for 5 minutes. Roll the dough into strips and cut into cylindrical sections, about 40g each. Press the dough sections into flat circles. Heat wok without using oil and fry both sides of pancake.

DEEP FRIED KING PRAWNS IN BATTER

6 king prawns (shells on)

Spiced salt mixture
salt (5 tbsps)
five-spiced powder (1 tbsp)

Batter
plain flour (100g)
baking powder (1$\frac{1}{2}$ tsp)
salt ($\frac{1}{2}$tsp)
cornflour (5 tsps)
oil (4 tsps)
lager (150g)

Clean and peel off the shells of the prawns, keeping the tails. Leaving the oil till last, mix together the ingredients for the batter, stirring well. Slice the prawns and flatten out before coating in the batter and frying. Serve with the spiced salt.

STEAMED WHOLE SEA BASS WITH GINGER AND SPRING ONION

whole sea bass (about 500g)
ginger (finely shredded)
spring onion (a few sprigs)
coriander leaves

light soy sauce (3 tbsp)
dark soy sauce (1 tbsp)
sugar (1 1/2 tsp)
pepper to taste
(these 4 to be mixed together)

Rub a little salt over the whole fish.
Put 3 sprigs of spring onion on a plate horizontally.
Put fish on top of the spring onion and place shredded ginger on top of the fish.
Add some oil and steam for 12 minutes.
Pour away the water from steaming.
Add freshly heated oil.
Garnish with fresh coriander, ginger and shredded spring onion.
Add some soy sauce mixture.

BEEF IN OYSTER SAUCE

sirloin beef (500g)

2 shitake mushrooms (sliced)

ginger (sliced)

2 carrots (sliced)

garlic

spring onion (cut into sections)

cornflour ($1/2$ tsp)

sesame oil

dark soy sauce

oyster sauce

sugar ($2/3$ tsp)

Slice beef thinly and season with salt, cornflour and oil.

Heat up wok with ginger, garlic and spring onion.

Stir fry the beef.

Add sliced shitake mushrooms and sliced carrots.

Add in seasoning, oyster sauce, sugar, dark Soy sauce, sesame oil and pepper and thicken with cornflour.

Photograph on page 143.

MARY WALKER

FISHERS

CHEF TEAM

BRENDAN SUGARS, MARY WALKER, RICHARD HILTON,
IAN ANTON RILEY, RUTH O'HARA AND GLYN SOMMERVILLE

'The great thing about working here is that we all have very different styles, and we are given the freedom to do what we want.'

I'm not exactly the Head Chef – there are six chefs here, I've just been here the longest (seven years now) and we've been together as a team for two years. It's a friendly, lively place. The great thing about working here is that we all have very different styles and we are given the freedom to do what we want. We all have different talents and strengths, and we learn from each other. Nobody knows it all.

The atmosphere is informal and we have lots of regular customers. It's not really a young person's place, although the staff are a young team. Fish is what we are known for and always has been. Some of our regulars have been coming here at least once a week, for years; they say they like the fact that they never have to eat the same meal twice. Obviously what we put on the menu is affected by what fish we can get hold of that day; that's part of the fun. We have to be creative. And fish is such a versatile food.

We use local suppliers, but not always local fish. It's just not possible, if you want to offer a good range of fish. But it does make such a difference having reliable suppliers. Fishers is in a great location. I've lived in Leith for fourteen years and it's changed so much – not all of it for the better. There are so many restaurants around here now, but it doesn't seem to make any difference to our business. Since Jake and Graeme took the place over eight years ago, the business has just grown and grown.

We're a casual bistro, where everyone is treated the same. That seems to be what people like. I remember when Tony and Cherie Blair turned up – a couple of years ago now – they just walked in. I think it was at the end of some official visit and they were just chilling out. They didn't seem to expect special treatment and they didn't get it! Another exciting but more dramatic event happened when Malmaison was being built next door; one of the hoardings blew off the building site and came shooting through the window here at Fishers. It was like something out of a movie, all in slow motion and glass everywhere. Fortunately no one was badly hurt.

The recipes we've chosen are varied, reflecting the broad menu we offer at Fishers – fish-oriented, but with lots of choice.

A WARM SALAD OF SEARED KING SCALLOPS;

BLACK PUDDING AND BANANA WITH A PASSION FRUIT, HABANERO CHILLI AND SPICED RUM DRESSING.

16 large king scallops (cleaned and trimmed)

300g good quality black pudding (in 15mm cubes)

2 semi-ripe bananas (cut diagonally into 1cm strips)

Sweet potato (approx. 300g, cut into long fine juliennes)

Salad:

1 heaped teaspoon pimenton (smoked paprika)

handful of coriander leaves

flour for dusting

heaped tsp brown sugar

20g melted butter

salt and pepper

I recommend a mixture of baby mustard, red chard, wild rocket and mizuna

Dressing:

1 habanero or Scotch bonnet chilli (deseeded and finely diced)

1 small red onion or 1/2 medium red onion (finely diced)

50ml spiced rum such as Morgans

30ml rice vinegar

50ml light olive or ground nut oil

pulp and seeds from 4 ripe passion fruits

zest and juice from 1 seville or similar orange

1 Dust the sweet potato julienne in the flour and smoked paprika. Deep fry till crisp. Season and set aside.

2 Grill the black pudding till crisp on the outside, set aside and keep warm.

3 Mix the dressing ingredients, season and set aside.

4 Heat a frying pan or skillet till smoking. Dot the scallops with butter and add to pan. Sear on one side for 30-40 seconds. Turn the scallops and add banana. Toss the pan. Add the sugar and remaining butter. Toss again until the scallops and banana are caramelised.

5 Transfer the scallops and banana to 4 plates of salad leaves. Add the black pudding. Divide the dressing over the 4 plates. Garnish with the coriander leaves and sweet potato juliennes.

A SEAFOOD STEW

WITH SHITAKE MUSHROOMS AND AROMATICS

500g shitake mushrooms

1 onion (finely chopped)

3cm ginger (finely chopped)

3 cloves of garlic

3 lime leaves

1 red chilli (finely chopped)

2 star anise

2 tbsp olive oil

1 tbsp sesame oil

2 litres vegetable stock

Suggested fish:

4 fresh crevettes

4 cleaned king scallops

200g fresh squid (cut into fine rings)

1kg fresh cleaned mussels

200g monkfish (cut into slices)

200g salmon (cut into slices)

Garnish:

4 spring onions (shredded)

50g fresh coriander (roughly chopped)

50g fresh basil (roughly chopped)

300g sliced pak choi

2 red chillies (finely chopped)

100g cooked egg noodles

250g shitake mushrooms (finely sliced)

Sweat half the shitake mushrooms with the chopped onion, chopped garlic, ginger, lime leaves, chilli and star anise in the olive and sesame oils. Add the vegetable stock and simmer for 30 minutes or until reduced by half.

Strain and discard the solids.

Return the stock to a wide poaching pan and bring to a gentle simmer. Add the remaining sliced mushrooms, fish and shellfish and gently poach for 4-5 minutes.

Meanwhile divide the warmed noodles and the garnish between 4 plates. Pour the stock on to the noodles, arrange the fish on top and serve.

BAKED FILLET OF HALIBUT
STUFFED WITH CEPS AND WRAPPED IN SMOKED BACON,
DRIZZLED WITH A NUTMEG SCENTED JUICE ON A
BED OF STEAMED JULIENNE VEGETABLES

4 x 175g halibut fillets

8 rashers smoked
   streaky bacon

20g flour

40g clarified butter

1 sprig of fresh thyme

700g ceps (cleaned)

20g butter

100ml double cream

10g breadcrumbs

1 egg

20g parsley and chives

salt and pepper

Sauce:

80ml white wine

5g ground nutmeg

10g honey

180ml brown stock (beef
   or veal)

Steamed Vegetables:

175g carrot

175g courgette

175g leeks

2 red peppers

Decoration:

Fresh herbs and 1
   poached langoustine

1 Pre heat oven to 180°C

2 To make stuffing: chop ceps, heads and stalks, into cubes. Heat a pan, melt 2g of butter in it and sauté the ceps. Season and add parsley and chives. When liquid has evaporated add the cream and breadcrumbs and cook for 3-4 mins. Take off the heat, mix the egg in thoroughly and put to one side.

3 Slice a pocket into the halibut fillets and fill with the cep mousse. Season the fish with black pepper and wrap in bacon. Lightly dust the halibut parcels with flour and pan fry in clarified butter until golden in colour. Add the thyme and cook in the oven for 8-10 mins, basting continuously. Remove the fish and keep warm. Discard the fat from the pan.

4 To make the sauce: deglaze the pan with wine, add nutmeg and honey and reduce by half. Add the brown stock and simmer for 5-10 mins. Strain the sauce and season. Cut the halibut into 3 slices and arrange on a plate. Drizzle with sauce and garnish with sprigs of fresh herbs (thyme, chives, flatleaf parsley) and poached langoustine.

5 Julienne and steam vegetables in steamer for 3-4 mins or until al dente.

MARY WALKER

LEMON CURD ICE CREAM

IN BRANDY SNAP BASKET, DRIZZLED WITH
A PASSION FRUIT AND VANILLA SYRUP

Lemon curd ice cream

1 litre double cream

1 jar lemon curd

6 egg yolks

175g castor sugar

2 lemons (juice and rind)

4 tbsp liquid glucose

1 vanilla pod

Brandy snap baskets

120g unsalted butter

225g castor sugar

120ml golden syrup

120g plain flour

Passion fruit and vanilla syrup

5 passion fruits

1 vanilla pod

450g castor sugar

570ml water

To make the ice cream:

Heat lemon curd, glucose and lemon juice in small pan. Whisk egg yolks and sugar until light and fluffy. Whisk double cream, seeds of vanilla pod and lemon rind together (to soft peaks). When the glucose mixture is cool pour into egg yolk mix and then add cream – make sure all three mixtures are well combined. Pour this mixture into a freezer container and freeze until firm, stirring every 30 minutes to break up the ice crystals.

To make the baskets:

Melt the butter and golden syrup. Place all the dry ingredients in mixing bowl. When the syrup mix is tepid, add to the dry ingredients and mix well. Place the batter mixture in the fridge for at least 1 hour. This mix can also be frozen. Preheat oven to Gas Mark 4 (180ºC). Take a silicon or teflon mat and place on a baking tray. Roll the mix into little balls in the palm of your hand and place 4 of these on the mat. Bake for about 5 minutes, until they have spread, gone lacy and turned a deep golden brown. Remove from the oven and allow to 'rest' for 1 minute – they need this time to set. Using a palette knife, lift and place immediately on a dariole mould (or small upturned pudding basin) – if the biscuits harden before you have time to shape them, return them to the oven and they will soften again. The baskets will stay crisp and fresh for a couple of days if stored in an airtight container.

To make the syrup:

Scrape the seeds from vanilla pod and cut the passion fruits in half. Place all the ingredients in a heavy-based pot and bring to the boil, boiling for 2-3 minutes. The passion fruit skins will turn the syrup pink. Skim off any scum that comes to the surface – this is just impurities released from the sugar. Remove from the heat and leave to cool. Store in a sealed container in the fridge.

MALCOLM WARHAM

36

'I like to focus on the main ingredients of a dish, to use local produce.'

I am a chef because of my dad, but I really wanted to be a footballer – in fact, I did have trials for Chester and Everton. I helped out in the kitchens for my dad, washing up and doing bits and pieces of cooking. That's how I fell in love with the job; I liked the pressure, and the camaraderie. My father was a chef in the Merchant Navy and then at a place called the Mollington Banastre in Chester. Through my dad, I got the opportunity of an interview at Gleneagles – I was there four years in the end. The training was hard, but good fun too. Well, it got better after the first six months, when all I was allowed to cook was the potatoes!

I've been here at 36 for four years. The style of the restaurant and the food we serve is minimalist, no fuss, but plenty of style. The food is modern Scottish with plenty of unexpected flavours, using spices and herbs from all over the world. I like to focus on the main ingredients of a dish and to use local produce. The recipes I've chosen use some of my favourite ingredients: salmon, smoked haddock, wild mushrooms, apples and goat's cheese.

One of my best experiences at 36 was when Sir Cliff Richard stayed at The Howard (36 is part of The Howard Hotel) when he was playing Heathcliff. He was such a nice man, so down to earth and not at all into being 'a celebrity'. He dined here quite a lot during his stay, and even took some of my chocolate brownies home with him. My worst experience was probably being summoned to speak to an Italian diner who disagreed with my Barley Risotto – he hadn't ordered it, but objected in principle to the idea of a risotto that used Scottish barley instead of Italian arborio rice!

I'm not particularly ambitious – apart from wanting to play for Liverpool, I want to stay healthy, and to continue to enjoy the pressure, and working with my team here at 36. I suppose I'd really like not to still be a chef by the time I'm 60 – that was where my dad went wrong, I think. I want to be running my own business – maybe a guest house in Troon, with my wife and three sons. A good place for golf courses – golf is another of my favourite things!

MALCOLM WARHAM

A TARTLET OF ACHILTIBUIE SMOKED HADDOCK AND WILD MUSHROOMS WITH

PARMESAN CRUST AND CUCUMBER RELISH

4 x 60mm shortcrust
    pastry tartlet cases

Filling

2 fillets, skin removed
    (I use Achiltibuie
    smoked haddock)

75g wild mushroom mix

25g butter

150ml double cream

pinch of cayenne pepper

$^1/_2$ tsp horseradish

pinch chopped parsley

Cucumber relish

500g cucumber

75g onion

$^1/_2$ red and $^1/_2$ yellow
    pepper

$^1/_2$ red chilli pepper

250ml white wine

$^1/_2$ tsp turmeric

1 tsp caraway seeds

150g soft brown sugar

$^1/_4$ tsp mixed spice

Crust

30g plain flour

30g butter

150ml milk

15g freshly grated
    Parmesan cheese

3 egg yolks

3 egg whites

Filling and crust

Prepare base first. Lightly poach the haddock in the milk for the crust and retain the milk.

Cook the mushrooms in the butter. Add the cream and cayenne pepper to this and add the smoked haddock, chopped parsley and horseradish and mix gently.

For the crust, melt the butter, stir in flour and gently cook for 1-2 minutes. Blend in the milk from the haddock and cook until it is thickened. Add the cheese and allow to cool slightly, then carefully beat in the egg yolks one by one. Whisk the egg whites until very stiff, then carefully fold them into egg yolk mixture.

Put a large spoonful of filling into pastry tartlet and top with the crust mix. Bake in a hot oven at Gas Mark 7/250°C for 12-15 minutes until golden brown.

Relish

Remove the seeds from cucumber and dice finely. Finely chop the onions and peppers. Cut the chilli pepper into fine juliennes, sprinkle all with a little salt. Leave for 30 minutes, then wash off salt.

To make syrup, put the white wine, sugar, caraway seeds, turmeric and spices into a saucepan and boil until a syrup consistency is reached, then pour over cucumber mix and infuse for two hours.

ROAST BREAST OF GUINEA FOWL
WITH A BALLOTINE OF THE LEG, FILLED WITH STORNOWAY
BLACK PUDDING AND AYRSHIRE BACON SET ON A CIDER SAUCE

2 x 1.5kg oven-ready guinea fowls

150g Stornoway black pudding

100g Ayrshire smoked bacon

2 eggs

20g parsley

15g chives

100ml double cream

2kg Maris Piper potatoes

1kg medium-sized carrots

200g butter

100g fine French beans

2 round Charlotte new potatoes

500ml cider sauce (1 litre veal jus, 1 litre dry cider, $^1/_2$ litre apple juice)

1 tsp ground cinnamon

olive oil

4 shallots

1 litre chicken stock

Remove legs and breasts from guinea fowl. Trim top of leg to expose bone. Pull back skin from leg, keep attached. Cut halfway down the drumstick through the bone. Remove meat from leg. Retain bone for sauce. Trim breasts. Keep chilled.

Place leg meat into food processor with the eggs. Pass through medium drum sieve. Place into a bowl. Dice black pudding and smoked bacon. Add to leg meat and fold in with cream, chives and parsley to make a farce. Pipe into the guinea fowl leg skin. Completely enclose the farce with the skin to form a cylindrical shape. Roll in cling film. Poach in chicken stock for approximately 25 minutes. Remove and keep warm.

Cook potatoes for mash. Put into piping bag and keep warm.

Prepare carrots into large tower, shape and cook (3 per person). Prepare beans and cook.

Slice Charlotte potatoes thinly on a mandolin. Arrange by overlapping, to form circles with a hollow in the middle. Gently fry both sides, until crisp.

Roast guinea fowl bones in hot oven. Drain, deglaze with chopped shallots. Add 1 litre of dry cider and $^1/_2$ litre of apple juice, and teaspoon ground cinnamon, reduce, then add 1 litre veal jus. Reduce, season and strain.

Roast guinea fowl supreme in 100g butter for approximately 12-15 minutes at Gas Mark 7/250ºC. Slice and arrange on plate.

Slice leg into 3. Arrange on plate, pipe potato on to plate, top with carrots, and beans. Pour sauce around and serve.

Photograph on page 159.

MALCOLM WARHAM

PAN FRIED ROSETTE OF SALMON

WITH A GOATS CHEESE AND PESTO RAVIOLI,
PROVENÇALE DRESSING

4 x 150g pieces salmon
fillet with skin and dark
flesh removed
100g good quality goat's
cheese

Pesto:

100g pine nuts (lightly
toasted)
25g brioche crumbs

50g basil leaves
30g Parmesan
2 cloves garlic
little olive oil to bind

Pasta:

200g 00 grade pasta flour
pinch salt
2 whole eggs
2 egg yolks

Dressing:

200ml extra virgin olive oil
3 cloves garlic (blanched)
2 lemons grated (zest and
juice)
15g thyme leaves
1 tbsp chives
1 tbsp chopped parsley
3 plum tomatoes (diced)
Maldon sea salt and pepper

Place basil and pine nuts into food processor. Pulse until well mixed and add other dry ingredients. Add salt and pepper and blend until smooth, adding olive oil a little at a time. Rest in fridge until firm.

Take 100g good quality goat's cheese, leaving skin on, and grate into a bowl. Mix with double the amount of pesto and form into a ball shape.

To prepare pasta: place flour and salt into food processor. Beat eggs together and add into machine slowly until a dough is formed. Take out and leave to rest for 1 hour.

Take 200g of ready prepared pasta and roll through a pasta machine to the finest setting. Cut out four 8cm circles and four 5cm circles. Place goat's cheese on the larger circles and place smaller circle on top, bringing the larger circle up to form ravioli shape. Seal with a little cold water if necessary. Cook in boiling water for 2-3 minutes and refresh in ice water until required for serving.

Dressing: Place olive oil into a Kilner jar (a glass jar with a rubber seal), adding the zest and juice from the lemons and the thinly sliced blanched garlic, along with the thyme leaves, salt and milled black pepper. Leave for 24 hours to infuse. Just before serving add the chives, parsley and diced tomato. Check seasoning and serve at room temperature.

To prepare salmon: make a cut in the fillet to open it out into one long strip, season and gently roll up to form rosette shape. Secure with a cocktail stick. In a non-stick frying pan with a little olive oil, seal the salmon on all sides, then cook in a hot oven, 250°C, for approximately 5-7 minutes. Take out and serve on top of stir-fried vegetables, with the reheated ravioli on top. Dress with vinaigrette and serve with new potatoes.

A TRIO OF '36' FAVOURITE DESSERTS

APPLE AND CALVADOS MOUSSE

9 egg yolks	150ml Calvados	**Italian Meringue:**
120g castor sugar	$1/4$ lemon juice	50ml Calvados
150ml cider	200g Bramley apples	150g sugar
$1/2$ vanilla stick	(peeled)	3 egg whites
20g milk powder	375ml whipped cream	
3 x $1/4$ leaves gelatine		

Beat the egg yolks and castor sugar together, to make the base for the crème anglaise. Mix together the cider, Calvados, lemon juice, vanilla and milk powder and bring to the boil. Pour the mixture onto the eggs and sugar. Mix well and pour back into the pan and thicken until the mixture coats the back of a wooden spoon. Add 3 $1/4$ leaves of gelatine to the mixture and leave to cool.

Make apple purée with 200g of peeled Bramley apples, and add to the crème anglaise.

To make the Italian Meringue: Boil the Calvados and sugar until a thick syrup is formed. Whisk the egg whites to the soft peak stage and add in the hot syrup. Carefully, and slowly, beat until cool.

When cool, fold the Italian Meringue into the crème anglaise, then gently fold in 375ml whipped cream.

Pour onto mould or tray. Leave to set for approximately 4 - 6 hours.

CARAMEL ICE CREAM

8 egg yolks	$1/2$ litre milk
250g castor sugar	$1/2$ litre cream

Beat the egg yolks and 100g sugar together, to make the base for the crème anglaise.

Mix together the milk and the cream and bring to the boil. Pour the mixture onto the eggs and sugar. Mix well and pour back into the pan and cook over a low heat until the mixture coats the back of a wooden spoon.

Boil remaining 150g sugar to a golden caramel.

Add the caramel to the crème anglaise and dissolve. Strain the mixture and leave to cool. Churn in a sorbetiere.

APPLE AND TARRAGON SOUFFLE

1.35kg Bramley apples (peeled, cored
   and cut into 2 cm dice)

100ml Calvados

100g castor sugar

Approx. 2tbsp cornflour to thicken

150g tarragon (chopped)

4 egg whites

To make the soufflé base: Cook apples with Calvados, 50g sugar and a little water in a heavy-bottomed pan until soft. Purée with a hand blender until smooth. Mix cornflour with a little apple juice. Bring purée back to the boil and thicken with the cornflour and apple juice mixture until a thin trail hangs from the whisk. Cook for a few minutes, and leave to cool.

   To make soufflé: Allow one egg white per person and approximately 50g of soufflé base. Whisk egg whites until they start to peak and slowly add in some of the remaining sugar to make a meringue (but not as sweet). Carefully fold the meringue into the apple mixture, adding the chopped tarragon. Spoon into a greased and sugared soufflé dish, cook in a hot oven (230ºC) for 10-15 minutes, until well risen. Serve straight away onto a plate garnished with the apple and Calvados mousse and the caramel icecream. Good luck!

GRAHAM WINTER & BLAIR GLEN

WINTER GLEN

'We work together, but separately — like a pantomime horse, really.'

Blair and I set up this restaurant in partnership in 1996.

We first worked together in the early 1990s, at the Scandic Crown in Edinburgh. We knew then that we worked well as a team. We work together, but separately – like a pantomime horse, really; the front needs the back and the back needs the front – but I won't say who is front or back! We can trust each other because we're working towards the same goal, which is looking after the customer. We do a lot of the work ourselves and we have a good team behind us. This isn't a concept restaurant. We're very 'hands on' and involved in the whole process. It's a confidence thing; we have the confidence to deliver good food with good service. This job is about performing and being motivated to aim for the best every time.

The site used to be a blacksmith's basement, but we took it on as a 'shell' from a developer. The location is ideal for what we wanted – a restaurant for business lunches, but also where people could come for lunch or dinner straight from a shopping trip or a visit to a gallery. We aim to create a relaxed atmosphere, a balance of the traditional and the modern, smart but informal; it's not possible to be over- or under-dressed as far as we're concerned. The food is good quality, the staff have personalities and the service is relaxed but efficient.

Our food is 'modern Scottish', which means using as many Scottish ingredients as possible, but with other influences. There are no tartan doilies at Winter Glen! We use Scottish beef, lamb, seafood and game, and add ethnic and unexpected touches. Taste and texture are the key features of any food – they are the things that last. Presentation is important too, but we try to use the natural colours of ingredients and how they work together in a dish. It's about getting everything in balance. The whole meal has to work as a dining experience, a kind of journey through tastes and textures.

Our ambition is to be the best at what we do. We've had great reviews here, which has made such a difference. But it's not been easy; we've had to learn some hard business lessons. That's the trouble with success, there are always people waiting in the wings, wanting to make the most of your work for their gain, or to trip you up. And they don't know the work it takes, or how hard it is.

SMOKED SALMON SAUSAGE

250g fresh salmon

100g smoked salmon

1 size 3 egg

100ml double cream

15g finely chopped dill

10g salt

10g freshly ground pepper

10g Dijon mustard

Place all ingredients into a food processor and 'blitz' to a very fine paste. This will take about 10-15 seconds (take care not to over-blend as this will cause the cream to separate).

To make the sausage, take a piece of cling film (about 25mm x 25mm) and place a large tablespoon of the mix in the middle. Draw the bottom of the cling film over the mix to form an envelope and, using both hands, press the mix back towards you to form a sausage shape. When you have the required shape, twist both ends in the opposite direction to seal the package.

Place the sausage on a metal tray and pour enough water on the tray to come about a third of the way up the side of the sausage. Bake in a moderate oven (around 190ºC) for about 10 minutes or until firm to the touch.

Allow to cool, remove cling film and keep refrigerated until needed.

When required, heat through in the oven or use a griddle to give a stripy effect.

We normally serve this dish with black pudding and olive mash, with a thread of dill butter, but I've also used a small amount of leek and potato gateaux and a couple of drops of red pepper coulis and some tapenade. Try a few combinations until you find something that suits your own taste.

GRIDDLED HALIBUT STEAK
WITH TOMATOES, BUTTER BEANS AND CHILLIES

4 x 150g Halibut Steaks

200g fresh tomatoes (skinned and deseeded)

100g dried butter beans (soaked
overnight)

100ml virgin olive oil

1 clove garlic (crushed)

25g coriander (chopped)

25g basil (chopped)

100ml chicken stock*

10g red chillies (finely chopped)

10g sea salt

10g freshly ground black pepper

200ml vegetable stock*

25g tomato purée

1 medium sized onion, finely chopped

* If using stock cubes, reduce salt

Go to your local fishmonger (remember him?) or find a fish quay and ask for four, nice, fresh, juicy halibut steaks with the bone in and the skin on. Take 25g of the olive oil and brush both sides of the steaks. Take half of the salt and pepper and season both sides again. Next take half the basil and coriander and sprinkle over the steaks. Cover with cling film and place in the bottom – the coldest part – of the fridge.

In a heavy-bottomed saucepan, over a medium heat, heat up the remaining olive oil. Then add the onion, garlic and chillies. Cook for a few minutes until the onion is soft, add tomato purée and cook for another minute, then drain the beans and add to the pan, mixing everything together before adding the tomatoes and stock. Bring to the boil and simmer gently for about one and a half hours, stirring from time to time and adding a little water if needed.

When the beans are soft enough to eat but still intact, add the rest of the herbs and the seasoning and remove from the heat to let the flavours infuse. When cool, store in the fridge until required.

To assemble the dish, warm the sauce through to a gentle simmer, taking care not to let it dry out. Next remove the steaks from the fridge and heat your new toy, the griddle, over a high heat. Then lay the steaks on by starting at the nearest point and then moving your hand away from you – watch the guy at the local chippy next time he puts the fish in!

Turn the heat down to about medium strength. After 5-6 minutes, turn the fish using a fish slice or wide palette knife and then cook for a further 5-6 minutes until the flesh just starts to come away from the bone. Plate up with whatever else you fancy (you've got the important bit right) and spoon over the sauce.

Photograph on page 167.

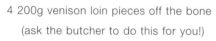

GRAHAM WINTER & BLAIR GLEN

PAN ROASTED LOIN OF VENISON

WITH BARLEY RISOTTO AND PORT
AND BEETROOT GRAVY

4 200g venison loin pieces off the bone
   (ask the butcher to do this for you!)
25ml vegetable oil
10g rosemary
1 garlic clove (crushed)
50g butter
10g salt
10g freshly ground black pepper

50ml port
100g cooked beetroot (1cm dice)
100ml beef stock
200ml chicken stock
150g pearl barley
1 medium sized onion (finely chopped)
50g redcurrant jelly

In a heavy-bottomed saucepan, melt 25g of the butter over a medium heat. Add two thirds of the onion and cook on until soft and clear. Next add about half the port, then the barley. Coat thoroughly with the butter and onions. Turn the heat up another third and slowly add the chicken stock. Bring gradually to the boil and simmer for about 20 minutes or until the barley is tender and most of the liquid has been absorbed.

Whilst the barley is cooking, heat a heavy-bottomed frying pan (cast-iron with a metal, ovenproof handle) over a high heat and add the vegetable oil and butter. When the butter starts frothing (but not burning) put in the venison. Whilst this is colouring on one side, coat the other with salt, pepper and rosemary and throw in the garlic (this will be discarded later). Turn up the meat when nicely coloured and place the pan in a preheated oven on the top shelf at 200ºC, for 10 minutes.

Remove the pan from the oven, lifting the meat from the pan and allowing it to 'rest' while you make the gravy. Remove the garlic from the pan, then place the pan over a medium heat. Throw in the remaining onion and cook in the pan juices for a couple of minutes, then add the last of the port, and the beef stock. Boil this down until reduced by half. Check the seasoning and finally whisk in the redcurrant jelly until it dissolves. Carve the meat and arrange it on warm plates together with vegetables of your choice. Spoon on the barley and lastly add the beetroot to the gravy before ladling it over the meat.

NB A good Burgundy, Claret or 'oaky' new world wine would go very well with this.

COLD RICE PUDDING
WITH PRUNES AND ARMAGNAC

For prune compote

200g good quality dried prunes

100ml boiling water

25g castor sugar

25ml Armagnac

For rice pudding

150g round pudding rice

375ml full fat milk

1 vanilla pod (cut in half lengthways)

25 g castor sugar

50ml whipping cream

$1/2$ tsp ground cinnamon

Place the prunes in a large saucepan and pour over the boiling water. Make sure all the prunes are submerged and leave to stand for 10 minutes. Place the pan over a low heat and gradually bring to a simmer. Stir in the sugar and cook until the liquor resembles a syrup. Remove from the heat and stir in the Armagnac – there will be sufficient heat to drive off the alcohol but leave the heavenly aroma and flavour of the Armagnac. Keep this to one side or in the fridge until you are ready to assemble the dish.

At Winter Glen we use Casterade Armagnac which is made by the oldest family-producer of Armagnac in France, but any decent brandy will do.

In a heavy-bottomed saucepan place all the ingredients for the rice pudding – except for the whipping cream – and place over a moderate heat. Stir periodically until it comes to the boil. Turn down the heat and very gently simmer, stirring occasionally to prevent the mix sticking to the bottom. This method differs from the conventional way of making rice pudding and requires a little more attention, as topping-up with milk during cooking may be needed (depending on the pan size and heat source). Carry on cooking (45-60 minutes) until the grains have burst and are cooked through, taking care to leave them with some texture. Place the rice into a large bowl or tray to cool as quickly as possible and refrigerate until needed.

To compile the dish, place the prunes over a moderate heat and add another wee splash of Armagnac at this stage, if you like. Add the whipping cream to the rice which should now be a 'workable' texture and fill the moulds on the plates, pushing down with the back a spoon. Spoon the prunes on top of the rice and serve immediately. You might like to garnish with a swirl of leftover cream or a splash of crème anglaise. I like it served with a glass of guess what?

EDINBURGH ON A PLATE CONTRIBUTORS

KALPNA
2-3 ST PATRICK SQUARE
EDINBURGH
EH8 9EZ
0131 667 9890

MALMAISON
ONE TOWER PLACE
LEITH
EDINBURGH
EH6 7DB
0131 555 6969

IGGS
15 JEFFREY STREET
EDINBURGH
EH1 1DR
0131 557 8184

LE CAFÉ ST HONORÉ
34 N.W. THISTLE STREET
   LANE
EDINBURGH
EH2 1EA
0131 226 2211

THE VINTNERS ROOMS
THE VAULTS
87 GILES STREET
LEITH
EDINBURGH
EH6 6BZ
0131 554 6767

**DUCK'S AT LE MARCHÉ
   NOIR**
2/4 EYRE PLACE
EDINBURGH
EH3 5EP
0131 558 1608

SKIPPERS BISTRO
1A DOCK PLACE
LEITH
EDINBURGH
0131 554 1018

THE ATRIUM
CAMBRIDGE STREET
EDINBURGH
EH1 2ED
0131 228 8882

CHANNINGS
15 SOUTH LEARMONTH
   GARDENS
EDINBURGH
EH4 1EZ
0131 315 2225

BLUE BAR CAFÉ
CAMBRIDGE STREET
EDINBURGH
EH1 2ED
0131 221 1222

THE POMPADOUR
THE CALEDONIAN HILTON
PRINCES STREET
EDINBURGH
EH1 4AB
0131 459 9988

**RESTAURANT AT THE
   BONHAM**
35 DRUMSHEUGH
   GARDENS
EDINBURGH
EH3 7RN
0131 623 9319

MARTINS RESTAURANT
70 ROSE STREET NORTH
   LANE
EDINBURGH
EH2 3DX
0131 225 3106

HALDANES
39A ALBANY STREET
EDINBURGH
EH1 6TW
0131 556 8407

INDIGO YARD
7 CHARLOTTE LANE
EDINBURGH
EH2 4QZ
0131 220 5603

RHODES & CO.
3-15 ROSE STREET
EDINBURGH
EH2 2YJ
0131 220 9190

HOWIES
29 WATERLOO PLACE
EDINBURGH
EH1 3BQ
0131 556 5766

BAMBOO GARDEN
57A FREDERICK STREET
EDINBURGH
EH2 1LH
0131 225 2382

FISHERS BISTRO
1 SHORE
LEITH
EDINBURGH
EH6 6QW
0131 554 5666

36
36 GREAT KING STREET
EDINBURGH
EH3 6QH
0131 556 3636

WINTER GLEN
3A DUNDAS STREET
EDINBURGH
EH3 6QG
0131 477 7060

LIST OF RECIPES